Binational Fisheries Management Plan
for Amistad Reservoir

United States Agency Contributors:
Texas Parks and Wildlife Department
National Park Service
US Fish & Wildlife Service

* Mexico Agency Contributors:
Secretaría de Agricultura, Ganadería, Desarrollo Rural,
Pesca y Alimentación.
Instituto Nacional de Pesca.
Comisión Nacional del Agua.
Secretaria de Turismo
SCT
Gobierno del Estado de Coahuila

* Mexico agencies contributed to the development of
the plan, but none have signed the final document.

BINATIONAL FISHERIES MANAGEMENT PLAN

Amistad National Recreation Area

National Park Service

Del Rio, Texas

Approved: _Alan W. Cox_   _8/3/06_
Superintendent   Date
Amistad National Recreation Area

Approved: _Philip P. Durocher_   _8/3/06_
Director, Inland Fisheries   Date
Texas Parks and Wildlife Department

Approved: _____
(Mexico is not a signatory at this time)   Date

Table of Contents

Table of Figures & Tables

BINATIONAL FISHERIES MANAGEMENT PLAN FOR AMISTAD RESERVOIR

INTRODUCTION

Reservoir history and its purposes

Amistad International Reservoir is a 26,300 hectare (65,000 acre) multi-purpose reservoir that impounds the Rio Grande River. The conservation pool level for the reservoir is set at 340.46 meters (1,117 foot) elevation. Surface area of water on the United States side totals 17,500 hectares (43,250 acres). Surface area of water on the Mexico side totals 8,800 hectares (21,750 acres). See Figure 1 for area map of the Amistad Reservoir.

Amistad Reservoir was created under the provisions of the Water Treaty of 1944 between the United States of America and Mexico and 22 USC 277d 13-16, Storage Dam – US and Mexico, approved July 7, 1960. The International Boundary and Water Commission (IBWC) acquired land up to the elevation of 348.87 meters (1144.3-foot mean sea level- msl) for the impoundment. The reservoir dam construction was completed in 1969.

The US purpose of the Amistad Reservoir is for water storage for municipal, industrial, and agricultural uses in south Texas. Amistad is a deep reservoir and contains less surface area, but more storage than Falcon Reservoir downstream. Water is released to Falcon Reservoir when domestic and industrial demands are high.

Within Mexico, the objectives for the construction of this reservoir are mentioned below in order of importance for the International Boundary and Water Commission for Mexico, known as CILA:
- Control flooding.
- Water storage.
- Generation of electricity.
- Agriculture.
- Fishing.
- Tourism.

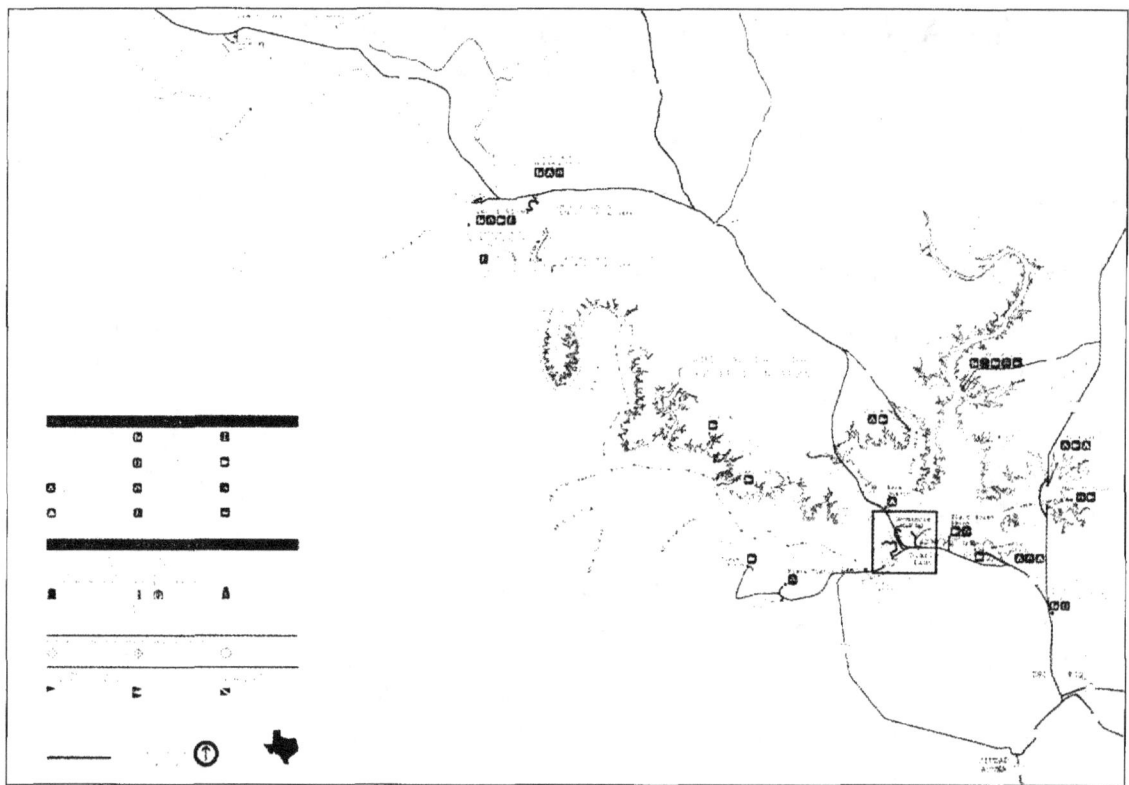

Figure 1. Area map of Amistad Reservoir

Environmental description

Amistad International Reservoir is located in a biological transition zone between the Chihuahuan desert, the Edwards Plateau (Balconian), and the southern Tamaulipan Brushland biotic provinces. This transition zone, coupled with the presence of limestone canyons and plateaus, creates an environment diverse in habitats.

The most common plant community surrounding the reservoir is the Blackbrush acacia brushland that occupies level plateau tops and gentle to steep slopes along drainages (Texas Natural Heritage Program, 1995). Common plants encountered around the reservoir include guajillo, mesquite, ocotillo, lechuguilla, and nopal. A highly disturbed plant community at Amistad occurs in the zone of the fluctuating reservoir water level. In this area, saltcedar *(Tamarix)*, roosevelt weed *(Baccharis)*, tree tobacco *(Nicotiana)*, and many species of grasses occur.

The primary fauna around Amistad includes white-tail deer, bobcats, javelina, cottontail rabbits, jackrabbits, wild turkey, scaled and bobwhite quail, white-wing doves, and morning doves. Puma and black bear are uncommon.

The reservoir was constructed on the Rio Grande and receives water from the Devils and Pecos Rivers. The Devils River drains an area of 6,928 square kilometers (4,305 square miles). This spring fed river is not regulated and is under very little influence by land use in the watershed, which is primarily ranches and small rural housing developments (Water Resources Scoping Report, 2001). The Pecos River flows from the

---

southern Rocky Mountains in New Mexico and drains a watershed of 70,796 square kilometers (44,000 square miles). The reservoir water tends to be clear and the temperature is low due to the depth of a large part of the reservoir, which averages 5 meters (16 feet), with depths reaching over 70 meters (230 feet). This causes the productivity index to be low.

The Conchos River is a major source of water for the Rio Grande; it joins the Rio Grande near Presidio, Texas, and Ojinaga, Chihuahua. The Conchos River hydrologic region (RH-24-A) includes an area of 75,442 square kilometers (46,774 square miles). This region covers the Conchos River drainage, in the State of Chihuahua and a small portion of the State of Durango. The northern boundary is the United States, northwest is RH-34 Chihuahua Basin), northeast is RH-24-B (Upper Rio Bravo/Grande), east is RH-35 (Coahuila and Chihuahua), south is RH-36 (Durango), and west are RH-9 (Sonora) and RH-10 (Sinaloa, Chihuahua and Durango).

Hydrologic Regions:
RH-34	Cuenca de Chihuahua.
RH-24-B	Alto Bravo.
RH-35	Coahuila y Chihuahua.
RH-36	Durango.
RH-9	Sonora.
RH-10	Sinaloa, Chihuahua, and Durango.

Types of activities that occur on the reservoir

Fishing

Fishing is one of the most popular recreational uses of the Amistad Reservoir within the US waters. The trophy bass fishery attracts around 150 organized bass tournaments annually. Most tournaments occur on the US side, but approximately 10 occur on the Mexico side. The number of fishing tournaments documented on the US side from 2002 to 2006 included the following: 2002= 155, 2003= 156, 2004= 138, 2005= 146, and 2006= 148. At times, the tournaments can bring as many as 600 boats on the water, with 4 or 5 tournaments occurring during the same weekend. Amistad Reservoir is considered to be one of the best trophy bass reservoirs in the world.

In Mexico the popularity of recreational fishing is growing. Sport fishing has increased steadily because the reservoir has been recognized as being good for this activity. This has caused the number of fishing permits issued and the number of fishing tournaments to increase during the last 10 years.

Other Activities

Other recreational activities on the reservoir includes recreational boating, such as wildlife viewing and visiting archeological pictographs, personal watercraft use, rental houseboat trips, hunting, and water skiing. Boat camping is also a popular activity along the reservoir shoreline.

Within Mexico, tourism created by the reservoir is important. The reservoir is suitable for water skiing, scuba diving, boating, visits to places that have pre-historic paintings, fossil hunting, camping, and observation of fauna. The shores of the reservoir have been registered as being suitable for hunting.

Commercial fishing

Within the Mexico portions of the reservoir there is a commercial fishery closely administered under the regulations and control of the government. There has been a steady effort to conserve this resource. The yearly catch has averaged 209 metric tons (230 tons). As of 2002, there were only two commercial fishing cooperatives with a total of 30 participants.

Current designations affecting the reservoir

US Designations

International Boundary and Water Commission- The enabling legislation for the construction, operation and maintenance of the Amistad Dam and Reservoir was authorized by the Act of Congress of July 7, 1960 (74 Stat. 360;22 USC 277d 13-16).

National Recreation Area Designation- Public Law 101-628 (11/28/90) designated land and waters on the US side of Amistad Reservoir as a National Recreation Area to be administered under the National Park Service.

State Park Area Designation- Seminole Canyon State Park and Historic Site is located on the Rio Grande arm of the Amistad Reservoir. The major points of interest are prehistoric pictographs.

Mexico Designations

None

US – Mexico Joint Designations/Treaty

Amistad International Reservoir was created under the provisions of the Water Treaty of 1944 between the United States of America and Mexico, approved on July 7, 1960.

Agency management plans that affect reservoir management

Texas Commission on Environmental Quality (TCEQ)

The United States and Mexico governments, through their respective sections of the International Boundary and Water Commission (IBWC), jointly operate and maintain the dam, dividing the costs in the same proportion as was determined in the Water Treaty of 1944, and effecting the division by each performing work corresponding to its share of the costs. Water releases are made from each country's share of the waters in conservation storage to meet its downstream requirements, as requested by the appropriate domestic authority. In the United States, the authority is the Texas Commission on Environmental Quality. Water releases for control of floods are determined jointly by the two Sections of the IBWC.

National Park Service

The General Management Plan for Amistad National Recreation Area provides general management oversight and direction to the NPS for Amistad NRA.

Texas Parks and Wildlife Department (Inland Fisheries)

The current fisheries management plan for Amistad Reservoir, dated June 31, 2000, was funded under the Federal Aid in Sport Fish Restoration Act; Project F30R, of the Texas Parks and Wildlife Department. Current management strategies include: 1) Statewide Harvest Regulations 2) Continue management and monitoring of the striped bass population under current regulations and 3) Stock fingerling striped bass annually based on water level, forage availability, fish condition, and estimated population size.

Secretaría de Agricultura, Ganadería, Desarrollo Rural, Pesca y Alimentación (SAGARPA)

Amistad Reservoir Official Mexican Law- In order to develop specific regulations for commercial and sport fishing for Amistad Reservoir, a socioeconomic study to gather the required data is needed.

Agreements between management agencies and groups

United States

1965 – The National Park Service entered into a Memorandum of Agreement with the IBWC on November 11, 1965 to provide for and manage recreation on the reservoir. By 1970, the reservoir was at full capacity, providing a recreational fishery for both Mexico and the United States.

1975 – A Memorandum of Understanding between The National Park Service and Texas Parks and Wildlife Department was signed which outlined the areas of responsibility of the two agencies for the management of fishery resources within the Texas national park units.

1975-1980 – Florida Bass Rearing Project: An agreement between the City of Del Rio and the Texas Parks and Wildlife Department. The City of Del Rio leased a hatchery facility near Del Rio. The TPWD biologist stationed in Del Rio managed the facility for the purpose of spawning and rearing Florida Bass fingerlings to be stocked into Amistad Reservoir. Approximately 200,000 Micropterus salmoides fingerlings were raised and stocked into Amistad annually under the agreement.

1980-1985 – Water Level Stabilization: An agreement was reached whereby the International Water and Boundary Commission made an effort to stabilize Falcon and Amistad Reservoirs during spawning periods to enhance largemouth bass production.

Mexico

Commercial fishing in Amistad Reservoir is regulated by the Federal Fishing Law and its regulations under Article 42. Those interested in obtaining commercial fishing permits must comply with the following requirements:

I.) Written request containing:

      a) target species name

      b) vessel name, description, and dimensions

      c) fishing area, base port, and launch locations

II.) Vessel registration certificate

III.) Production and operation plan.

Since 1980, the Amistad Fishing Cooperative has renewed their permit every two years in compliance with the established rules.

Article 45 requires fish cooperatives to:

- only catch authorized species within areas determined by the Secretary.
- fish only with approved boats and methods.
- assist with the preservation of the environment and conservation of species so as to support stocking programs in natural habitats according to the terms and conditions of the Secretary.
- present to the Fisheries Subdelegation a monthly report on each cooperative member's catch.

The Amistad Fishing Cooperative includes 36 members and 35 vessels. The minimum catch size is 25 centimeters (9.85 inches) and a commercial fishing permit is required, along with approved fishing methods.

Binational management plan purpose and need

There are two US Federal agencies and one US State agency, one Federal Mexico agency, one Mexico Federal National Fisheries Commission, and one State Mexico Agency with interest and management responsibility for the fishery resources of Amistad Reservoir. There is no common management plan in place. Both the US and Mexico have promoted and regulated fish harvest, and carried out independent fish stocking practices in the past with no coordinated management goals. This plan was developed to provide a mechanism for coordination in fisheries management actions among the state of Texas, the US National Park Service, the US Fish and Wildlife Service, the Secretaria de Agricultura, Ganaderia, Desarrollo Rural, Pesca y Alimentacion (SAGARPA) and Comisión Nacional de Pesca (CONAPESCA). Each of these agencies has responsibilities for management and use of the fishery resources of the reservoir and their legislated mandates for management must be accommodated. In the past, different regulations, management philosophies, and missions among these government entities have led to the absence of a unified approach to managing the reservoir fisheries and potentially conflicting management actions. This plan seeks to provide a more unified approach which hasn't existed in the past. Through a Binational Fisheries Management Plan, coordinated management of fish stocks, consistent and complementary harvest regulations, coordinated biological and chemical monitoring, and coordinated fish stocking and habitat management actions can begin to occur. This plan attempts to lay out agreements in regard to communication protocols, management goals and strategies, law enforcement assistance, joint public education and information efforts, public access, and important scientific studies to be undertaken.

Process used to develop cooperative plan

On October 2, 1998, natural resource staff from Amistad NRA and fisheries management staff from SEMARNAP and INP met on the shores of Amistad Reservoir near Playa Tlaloc, Mexico. The visit was arranged to observe cooperative commercial fisheries activities and learn about the monitoring project SEMARNAP was conducting on the cooperatives. Many questions and requests for information were shared and developed between the participants, showing a need for improved communication between management agencies. Over the following six months, it was decided by area State and Federal managers that a goal to improve the management of the shared fisheries resources for Amistad Reservoir was needed.

During 1999, natural resource staff from Amistad NRA, staff from the Water Resource Division for the NPS, and staff from SEMARNAP in Ciudad Acuña, Mexico, developed a proposal to fund the creation of a Binational Fisheries Management Plan. The proposal received a two year funding approval through the United States Department of the Interior US-Mexico Border XXI program initiative for fiscal years 2000 and 2001.

On September 19th and 20th, 2000, the first fishery meeting was held in Ciudad Acuña, Mexico. Representatives from the United States and Mexico fisheries management agencies met to share mandates, problems in the management of fisheries at

Amistad Reservoir, and future needs. Participants left the first meeting with an agreed goal to "Improve the management of Amistad Reservoir fisheries through inter-agency and international cooperation." Three objectives were developed to accomplish this goal: (1) develop a binational fisheries management plan, (2) establish channels of communication between participating agencies, and (3) identify and address the educational needs of all constituents. A working group was formed to develop the plan. A site visit to observe the fish cooperatives on the Mexico side of Amistad Reservoir was conducted by participants to learn monitoring protocols conducted by SAGARPA.

On February 6th and 7th, 2001, the working group met for the second time in Del Rio, Texas, to continue in the formulation of a fisheries management plan. Presentations by experts on fisheries issues were delivered; a draft outline of the plan was presented and improved amongst participants, and fisheries plan writing assignments were given to agency participants. A site visit to Amistad NRA visitor infrastructure was provided to participants at the end of the meeting.

On May 23 and 24, 2001, a third meeting of the working group was held in Saltillo, Mexico, to continue in the formulation of the fisheries plan and to conduct a site visit to the Mexico Federal fish hatchery "La Rosa" where more than 9 million hatchlings are raised of four species (carp, tilapia, bass and catfish). Attendees received a tour and explanation of fish production activities. The meeting was spent completing initial draft sections of the plan and agreeing formally on draft goals, objectives, and tasks for the plan.

On November 27 and 28, 2001, a fourth meeting of the working group was held in Ciudad Acuña, Mexico, to continue in the formulation of the fisheries plan. The meeting was spent reviewing the draft document for corrections and finalizing plan formation.

AGENCY MISSION STATEMENTS

United States

National Park Service

The Mission of the National Park Service at Amistad National Recreation Area is stated in the strategic plan, as follows: "The National Park Service is committed to protecting the scenic, scientific, cultural, and other values that contribute to the public enjoyment of lands and waters at Amistad National Recreation Area. We are dedicated to conserving unimpaired the natural and cultural resources and values for the education and inspiration of this and future generations."

US Fish and Wildlife Service

The mission of the US Fish and Wildlife Service is to work with others, to conserve, protect and enhance fish, wildlife, and plants and their habitats for the continuing benefit of the American people. The Service helps protect a healthy environment for people, fish and wildlife, and helps Americans conserve and enjoy the outdoors and our living treasures. The Service's major responsibilities are for migratory birds, endangered species, certain marine mammals, and freshwater and anadromous fish.

Texas Parks and Wildlife Department

The mission of Texas Parks and Wildlife Department is to manage and conserve the natural and cultural resources of Texas and to provide hunting, fishing and outdoor recreation opportunities for the use and enjoyment of present and future generations.

The mission of Texas Parks and Wildlife Department Inland Fisheries Division is to provide the best possible fishing while protecting and enhancing freshwater aquatic resources.

> **Goal:** Make Texas freshwater fishing the best in the world.

International Boundary & Water Commission

Our mission is to provide environmentally sensitive, timely, and fiscally-responsible boundary and water services along the United States and Mexico border region. We pledge to provide these services in an atmosphere of Binational Cooperation and in a manner responsive to public concerns.

Mexico

SAGARPA

The current mission of SAGARPA is to achieve the development of a new rural society based on sustainable growth in the sectors of agriculture and fisheries with continuing training and improvement that allow productivity, profitability, and competition in fisheries, agriculture, among other natural resources.

INP

The mission of the Instituto Nacional de la Pesca is to supply the scientific and technical data that determine the management standards to optimize the utilization of fisheries resources.

CONAPESCA

CONAPESCA's mission is to administer, with quality and openness, a sustainable utilization of fisheries and aquatic resources, to improve their production, distribution, and consumption to support a comprehensive increase of means of production, and to improve the diet of the Mexican people.

CAN

The mission of the Comisión Nacional del Agua is to administer and preserve the nation's waters, and with society's involvement, to achieve a sustainable use of this resource.

State of Coahuila

The mission of the government of Coahuila is to achieve harmonious improvement in agriculture, ranching, and forestry activities; to protect its sustainability, take advantage of its large production potential, and improve its efficiency and profitability by incorporating the producers' determined involvement to create necessary technological, economic, and social advance.

See appendix IV for agency management authorities and policies.

HISTORY OF FISHERY MANAGEMENT ON THE RESERVOIR

State of Texas

Species managed

Through agreement with the National Park Service, the State of Texas has had the primary responsibility for managing fishery resources within the US portion of the reservoir. Texas has stocked and taken management actions to sustain the following major sports (game) fish within the reservoir:

Largemouth bass (*Micropterus salmoides*)
Smallmouth bass (*Micropterus dolomieu*)
Channel catfish (*Ictalurus punctatus*)
Blue catfish (*Ictalurus furcatus*)
Flathead catfish (*Pylodictis olivaris*)
Striped bass (*Morone saxatilis*)
White bass (*Morone chrysops*)
White Crappie (*Pomoxis annularis*)
Walleye (*Stizostedion vitreum*)
(Note—Walleye have not been collected for several years)

Stocking history

Texas Parks and Wildlife Department, Inland Fisheries Division, has a long history of stocking efforts within Amistad Reservoir and recorded stockings are presented in Table 1. Stocking was initiated in 1967 when the reservoir was just being completed and beginning to fill with water. Initially, largemouth bass, channel catfish, and white crappie were stocked. Blue catfish were then introduced in 1971 and striped bass in 1974. In 1975, smallmouth bass, walleye, and hybrid striped bass were first introduced. The last species to be introduced were the northern pike and muskellunge in 1976. Since their initial introductions, northern pike, muskellunge and blue catfish have not been stocked by the US. White Crappie were stocked a second time in 1989 but have not since been stocked. Since 1975, all largemouth bass stocked by the US have been of the Florida strain. Since 1997, only striped bass and largemouth bass have been stocked into the reservoir by TPWD. Other game fish species, except walleye, have been self-sustaining through natural reproduction.

Standardized fishery assessment surveys are routinely conducted to determine reproduction, recruitment, growth, condition, and relative abundance of fish populations. These parameters, in conjunction with established stocking criteria and current reservoir water level and habitat conditions, are used to formulate annual stocking recommendations.

Table 1. Texas Parks and Wildlife Department stocking history of Amistad Reservoir, Texas

Size categories are ADL for adult, FGL for fingerling, and FRY for fry.

English	Español	Scientific/Científico	Year/ Año	#	Size/ Tamaño
Northern Pike	Lucio del norte	Esox lucius	1976	1,030,305	FRY
Muskellunge	Lucio	Esox masquinongy	1976	700	FGL
Blue Catfish	Bagre azul	Ictalurus furcatus	1971	5,445	FGL
White Crappie	Carpa blanca	Pomoxis annularis	1968	100	ADL
			1989	144,491	FGL
StripedXWhite Bass	Róbalo rayado blanco	Morone hybrid	1975	171,300	FGL
			1976	173,662	FGL
			1982	1,270,000	FGL
Walleye	Walleye	Stizostedion vitreum	1975	5,250,000	FRY
			1976	5,100,000	FRY
			1977	2,033,000	FRY
			1978	5,000,000	FRY
Smallmouth Bass	Róbalo boca chica	Micropterus dolomieu	1975	100,000	FGL
			1976	200,000	FGL
			1978	164,750	FGL
			1983	200,500	FGL
Largemouth Bass	Róbalo verde	Micropterus salmoides	1967	1,053,750	FGL
			1968	928,425	FGL
			1969	810,700	FGL
			1971	446,660	FGL
			1972	100	ADL
			1973	1,050	ADL
			2004	42,077	FGL
			2005	289,666	FGL
Channel Catfish	Bagre de canal	Ictalurus punctatus	1967	22,650	FGL
			1968	317,695	FGL
			1969	77,025	FGL
			1971	8,000	FGL
			1972	10,100	FGL
			1973	50,550	FGL
Florida Largemouth Bass	Róbalo verde florida	M. salmoides	1975	52,000	FGL
			1976	260,000	FGL
			1977	674,220	FGL
			1978	596,000	FGL
			1979	450,000	FGL
			1980	214,700	FGL
			1992	507,075	FGL
			1996	130,768	FGL
			1997	500,943	FGL
			2004	552,648	FGL
			2006	4,519	FGL
Striped Bass	Róbalo rayado	Morone saxatilis	1974	212,616	FGL
			1976	62,992	FGL
			1977	693,107	FGL
			1978	204,891	FGL
			1979	255,000	FGL
			1980	12,000	FGL
			1982	101,000	FGL
			1984	649,289	FGL
			1986	180,770	FGL
			1988	850,000	FGL
			1991	332,371	FGL
			1992	339,369	FGL
			1993	657,937	FGL
			1994	1,316,638	FGL
			1995	100,259	FGL
			1997	67,463	FGL
			1998	67,885	FGL

	1999	67,800	FGL
	2000	436,717	FGL
Striped Bass (cont.)	2002	133,800	FGL
	2004	99,311	FGL
	2005	318,908	FGL
	2006	120,085	FGL

A list of stocking criteria by species is provided in Appendix V.

Harvest regulation history

The history of the state of Texas regulatory actions in the management of fish stocks at Amistad Reservoir are shown in Table 2. Regulations on the harvest of some species have been in place since the reservoir was first filled in 1969.

Table 2. Progression of US harvest regulations for game fish at Amistad Reservoir

English	Español	Scientific/Científico	Year/ Año	MIN LENGTH/ TALLA MINIMA	BAG LIMIT/ LIMITE POR BOLSA
White Crappie/ Black Crappie	Carpa blanca/ Carpa negra	Pomoxis annularis/ Pomoxis nigromacultatus	1969	none/ninguno	none/ninguno
			1986-87	none/ninguno	25
			1990-91	10in/25.4cm	25
			current/actual	same/mismo	same/mismo
White Bass	Róbalo rayado blanco	Morone chrysops	1969	none/ninguno	none/ninguno
			1988-89	10in/25.4cm	25
			current/actual	same/mismo	same/mismo
Walleye	Walleye	Stizostedion vitreum	1969	none/ninguno	5
			1987-88	16in/40.6cm	10
			1988-89	16in/40.6cm	5
			1999-00	2 <16in/40.6cm	5
			current/actual	same/mismo	same/mismo
Smallmouth Bass	Róbalo boca chica	Micropterus dolomieu	1969	none/ninguno	none/ninguno
			1991-92	14in/35.6cm	5
			current/actual	same/mismo	same/mismo
Largemouth Bass	Róbalo verde	Micropterus salmoides	1969	10in/25.4cm	10
			1986-87	14in/35.6cm	5
			current/actual	same/mismo	same/mismo
Channel Catfish/ Blue Catfish	Bagre de canal/ Bagre azul	Ictalurus punctatus/ Ictalurus furcatus	1969	none/ninguno	25
			1978-79	9in/22.8cm	25
			1995-96	12in/30.5cm	25
			current/actual	same/mismo	same/mismo
Spotted Bass	Róbalo moteada	Micropterus punctulatus	1969	none/ninguno	none/ninguno
			1991-92	12in/30.5cm	5
			2000-01	none/ninguno	5
			current/actual	same/mismo	same/mismo
Striped Bass	Róbalo rayado	Morone saxatilis	1969	none/ninguno	none/ninguno
			1978-79	none/ninguno	3
			1979-80	none/ninguno	5
			1988-89	18in/45.7cm	5
			current/actual	same/mismo	same/mismo
Flathead catfish	Bagre piltontle	Pylodictis olivaris	1969	none/ninguno	5
			1978-79	9in/22.8cm	5
			1992-93	18in/45.7cm	5
			1993-94	24in/70.0cm	5
			1995-96	18in/45.7cm	5
			current/actual	same/mismo	same/mismo

Possession limit is twice the statewide daily bag limit. There are no exceptions to the statewide possession limits in fresh water. Fish stored by a person at their permanent residence do not apply to their possession limit.

Mexico

Species managed

In Amistad Reservoir there are sport and commercial fisheries. The commercial fishery catch focuses on catfish, carp, tilapia, freshwater drum, bigmouth buffalo, shad, and gar. The sport fishery focuses on black bass and striped bass. Commercial fisherman can catch all of the above mentioned species, with the exception of black bass and striped bass which are reserved for recreational or sport fishing. Both commercial and sport fish species are promoted for management. The major species targeted by each of these fisheries is presented in Table 3.

Table 3. Commercial and sport fish of Amistad Reservoir

NOMBRE COMúN/ COMMON NAME	NOMBRE CIENTÍFICO/ SCIENTIFIC NAME	ORIGEN/ ORIGIN
Especies Comerciales/Commercial Species:		
Besugo, Tambor, Sargo/Freshwater Drum	*Aplodinotus grunniens*	Nativo/Native
Potranaca/River Carpsucker	*Carpiodes carpio*	
Chupon blanco/White Sucker	*Catostomus comersonni*	Nativo/Native
Matalote, Búfalo, Dorado/Bigmouth Buffalo	*Ictiobus ciprinellus*	Nativo/Native
Carpa Comun/Common Carp	*Cyprinus carpio*	Introducida/Introduced
Cuchilla, Shad, Alosa/Gizzard Shad	*Dorosoma cepedianum*	Nativo/Native
Tilapia, Mojarra Africana/Tilapia	*Tilapia spp*	Introducida/Introduced
Sardina brillo de oro/Golden Shiner	*Nothemigonus crysoleucas*	Nativo/Native
Sardina, Piscardo cabeza grande/Fathead Minnow	*Pimephales promelas*	Nativo/Native
Especies Comerciales y Deportivas/ Commercial and Sport Species:		
Bagre Azul/Blue Catfish	*Ictalurus furcatus*	Nativo/Native
Bagre Blanco/White Catfish	*Ictalurus catus*	Nativo/Native
Bagre cabeza de toro negro/Black Bullhead	***Ameiurus melas***	Nativo/Native
Bagre cabeza de toro café/Brown Bullhead	*Ameiurus nebulosas*	Nativo/Native
Bagre de canal, Pez gato catfish/Channel Catfish	*Ictalurus punctatus*	Nativo/Native
Piltontle/Flathead Catfish	*Pylodictis olivaris*	Nativo/Native
Catan, Pejelagarto/Longnose Gar	*Lipisosteus osseus*	Nativo/Native
Catan/Spotted Gar	*Lipisosteus oculatus*	Nativo/Native
Mojarra de agallas azules/Bluegill	*Lepomis macrochirus*	Nativo/Native
Mojarra pecho amarillo/Redear Sunfish	*Lepomis microlopus*	Nativo/Native
Especies Deportivas/Sport Species:		
Lobina Negra, Robalo verde/Largemouth Bass	*Micropterus salmaoides*	Nativo/Native
Lobina boca chica y grande/Smallmouth Bass	*Micropterus dolomieu*	Nativo/Native
Lobina moteada/Spotted Bass	*Micropterus punctulatus*	Nativo/Native
Lobina rayada, robalo rayado/Striped Bass	*Morone saxatilis*	Introducida/Introduced
Lobina rayada hibrida/White Bass	*Morone chrysops*	Introducida/Introduced
Lobina de florida, Floridae/Florida Bass	*Micropterus salmoides floridaus*	Introducida/Introduced
Robaleta Negra, Crappie/Black Crappie	*Pomoxis nigromaculatus*	
Robaleta Blanca, Crappie/White Crappie	*Pomoxis annularis*	
Robalo dienton, lucio perca walley/Walleye	*Stizosteidon vitrium*	Introducida/Introduced

Source: Orbe-Mendoza y Hernández-Montaño, 2000.

Stocking History

Mexico initiated stocking activities in Amistad Reservoir in 1994 as part of a statewide aquaculture program to develop and improve the commercial fishing industry and to provide alternative food sources to the people of Coahuila. Recorded stockings by SEMARNAP and SAGARPA are shown in Table 4.

Bass and catfish have been the subject of the majority of the stocking efforts, with bass planting each year since 1994. Catfish were stocked in 1995, 1998, 2000 and 2001. Tilapia were stocked in 1997 and 1998, however there has not been much impact since it is a tropical species that doesn't adequately develop in a deep, cold-water reservoir. It's important to note that the stocking was with fingerlings between 4 and 8 inches.

Table 4. Mexican fish stocking data from 1994-2002 for Amistad Reservoir, Ciudad Acuña, Subdelegación de Pesca del Estado de Coahuila

YEAR	SPECIES				
	BASS	CATFISH	TILAPIA	CARP	TOTAL
1994	30,000				30,000
1995	40,000	80,000			120,000
1996	30,000	15,000			45,000
1997	19,500	26,000	10,000	20,000	75,500
1998	50,000	30,000	21,000		101,000
1999	25,000				25,000
2000	5,000				5,000
2001	16,500	7,000		3,000	26,500
2002	7,000	30,000			37,000
TOTAL	223,000	188,000	31,000	23,000	465,000

Harvest regulation history

Amistad Reservoir is identified nationally and internationally as a symbol of collaboration and harmonious coexistence. The building of this reservoir at the end of the sixties made possible the formation of a geographic water resource, which represents a patrimony and a resource for the economic, social and cultural development of the region.

Commercial fishing in Amistad Reservoir began in 1980 with the formation of the cooperative La Amistad, which was followed later by the collective fishing farm *Unidad de Producción Pesquera Ejidal "Alfredo V. Bonfil"* and whose activities are regulated by the current fishing law. Gutting and filleting are the processing activities that these two fishing organizations do; in the case of carp, there is the additional option of slices with spines.

The manual of procedures for fishing regulations includes the following guidelines for fisheries management.

For commercial fishing:

- Review existing permits and issue permits to individuals and institutions that fulfill all legal requirements.
- Report upon landing: fish sizes, the catch quantity, and fish behavior in the reservoir.
- Report monthly economic revenue generated through fishing.
- Keep updated records of the size of the population engaged in fishing, and of the existing fleets and infrastructure.

For sport fishing:

- Issue permits to individuals who ask for them and who fulfill all legal requirements.
- Authorize sport fishing tournaments requested by clubs.

Cooperative Accords Reached in the Past

To avoid conflicts between the interested parties, agreements have been reached with the cooperatives and clubs about fishing in the reservoir.

In 1980, the former Secretaría de Pesca through the Coahuila delegation created an agreement between the commercial fishermen in the fishing cooperatives and the sport fishermen from different fishing clubs in order to improve the reservoir fishery. The following agreements were made.

The Fishing Cooperatives:

- Must display and renew the 2-year commercial fishing permit from the Secretaría de Pesca.
- The authorized fishing areas are from Buoy 9 to where the reservoir meets the Rio Grande, as well as the Mexican waters to 10km (6 miles) above the mouth of the Pecos River.
- Commercial fishing will only take place from Monday through Friday.
- Commercial fishing is authorized for all species except for bass, which are reserved for sport fishing.
- The Secretary will be notified of catch volumes each month.
- Assist and supply samples for scientific studies on species of commercial interest and temporary capture of sport species for these studies.

Sport Fisherman:

- Will have an individual sport fishing license and boat permit issued by the Secretaría de Pesca.
- May only have tournaments Saturdays and Sundays.
- May only use authorized fishing methods.
- The possession limit per person in two days is five each per species, with no more than three different species per day, and may reach the three day limit on Saturday and Sunday.

- Fishing clubs must receive approval from the Subdelegación de Pesca and may only fish Saturdays and Sundays.
- Tournament results will be sent to the Secretary.

The Subdelegación de Pesca:
- Will ensure the cooperatives and sport fishermen comply with the established rules.
- Issue commercial and sport fishing permits.

This agreement is in effect from 1980 to this date and ensures a harmonious relationship between commercial and sport fishermen through the contracted rules.

CURRENT STATUS AND CONDITION OF THE FISHERY RESOURCES

Species composition, abundance and distribution

The major sport fishes found in Amistad include largemouth bass *(Micropterus salmoides)*, channel catfish *(Ictalurus punctatus)*, white bass *(Morone chrysops)* and striped bass *(Morone saxatilis)*. All of these species are fairly abundant throughout the reservoir proper. Smallmouth bass *(Micropterus salmoides)* are fairly abundant in the Devils River and in the Devils River arm of the reservoir, with a lesser abundance found in the reservoir proper. White crappie *(Pomoxis annularis)*, a species stocked only twice, are found to be limited in abundance and have been documented primarily up the Devils River arm of the reservoir. Striped bass and white bass are more concentrated up the river portions of the reservoir during spring spawning runs.

Sunfish, including bluegills *(Lepomis macrochirus)*, redbreast sunfish *(Lepomis auritus)*, green sunfish *(Lepomis cyanellus)*, and warmouth sunfish *(Lepomis gulosus)* are abundant throughout the reservoir along the rocky shoreline. Other sunfish present, although never stocked, include longear sunfish *(Lepomis megalotis)* and redear *(Lepomis microlophus)* sunfish.

The most abundant forage (baitfish) includes gizzard shad *(Dorosoma cepedianum)* and threadfin shad *(Dorosoma petenense)*. These fish are found throughout the reservoir proper as well as up the river arms.

Two cichlids, Rio Grande cichlid *(Cichlasoma cyanoguttatum)* and Blue tilapia *(Oreochromis aureas)* are found in limited numbers throughout the reservoir but may be found concentrated around springs in the reservoir.

Amistad has three major watersheds on the American side which contribute to the diversity of aquatic plant and animal life. The Rio Grande is the largest, followed by the Pecos River drainage and the Devils River drainage.

A complete list of fish species known to occur within Amistad Reservoir and in-flow areas based on Texas Parks and Wildlife Department observations is presented in Appendix I.

Threatened and endangered species

Goodenough Spring was inundated under Amistad Reservoir during its initial filling. This large, natural spring was the home of the only population of Amistad gambusia (*Gambusia amistadensis*), a small fish in the Poeciliidae (livebearer) family. The species was listed as federally endangered in 1980 (45 FR 28721) because of the loss of its habitat at Goodenough Spring under the reservoir and the only known populations were being held in captivity. By 1984, the captive reserves had died out or were lost to hybridization with the common mosquitofish, resulting in the extinction of the species. Amistad gambusia was removed from the Federal endangered list in 1987 (45 FR 28721) after being confirmed as extinct.

The Devils River minnow (*Dionda diaboli*) is a small, native fish in the Cyprinidae (minnow) family. Its historic range included the Devils River from near the mouth of the Rio Grande to the headwater springs near Juno. As a result of the construction of Amistad Reservoir and the subsequent changes in the aquatic habitat and fish community, the species has apparently been extirpated from downstream of Dolan Falls in the Devils River. Ongoing efforts to document the current distribution of the Devils River minnow may expand the current range in the Devils River. The only other confirmed locations of this species in Texas are Pinto Creek in Kinney County and San Felipe Creek in the City of Del Rio. Devils River minnow was listed, without critical habitat designated, as a Federally threatened species in October 1999 (56 FR 58804). The US Fish and Wildlife Service completed a Recovery Plan in September of 2005. There is an existing Conservation Agreement for this species between the US Fish and Wildlife Service, Texas Parks and Wildlife Department and the City of Del Rio.

Interior least terns (*Sterna antillarum*) are small 20.3 – 22.9 cms (8 –9 inches) shorebirds that breed in isolated areas along the Missouri, Mississippi, Ohio, Red, and Rio Grande river systems. Their wintering sites include coastal areas of Central and South America. From late April to August, terns nest on barren to sparsely vegetated sandbars along rivers, sand and gravel pits, or lake and reservoir shorelines. Interior least terns have been documented breeders at the Amistad Reservoir since 1989. Preferred nesting habitat is found on islands with no vegetation or fire ants. These habitats occur during spring draw down of the reservoir, when islands emerge from inundation. The least tern has been listed as a Federal endangered species since 1985 (50 FR 21784).

Prior to the construction of Amistad Reservoir, a number of rare fishes may have inhabited the Rio Grande, Pecos and Devils Rivers that are now recognized as threatened or endangered by the State of Texas. These species, now likely extirpated from the area, include: shovelnose sturgeon *(Scaphirhynchus platorynchus)*; Rio Grande silvery minnow *(Hybognathus amarus)*; Rio Grande bluntnose shiner *(Notropis simus simus)*; proserpine shiner *(Cyprinella proserpina)*; blue sucker *(Cycleptus elongates)*; Conchos pupfish *(Cyprinodon eximius)*; blotched gambusia *(Gambusia senilis)*; and Rio Grande darter *(Etheostoma grahami)*. Of these eight State-listed species, three (shovelnose sturgeon, Rio Grande silvery minnow, and blotched gambusia) are considered extirpated from Texas, and the Rio Grande bluntnose shiner is considered extinct.

See NOM-059-ECOL-1994, that lists the plants and wildlife species, terrestrial and aquatic, that are rare, endemic, threatened, in danger of extinction, and subject to special protection in Mexico (DOF. 16-V-94).

The major extinct species on the Mexican side, specifically in the State of Coahuila are:

- Mexican wolf
- Pronghorn antelope
- Bison*
- Grizzly bear
- Elk*
- Bighorn sheep

* Reintroduced species in the State of Coahuila

Table 5. Changes in Fish Species in the Río Sabinas, Múzquiz, Coahuila between 1959 and 1994

	'59 LVG	'78 SCB	'85 GAG	'// //	'94a SCB	'94m SCB	'94b SCB	
Notropolis saladonis	R			++				EXTINCT
Gambusia marshi	R			//				IMPACTED
Ictalurus lupus	R	R		//				IMPACTED
Notropus jemezanus			R	//				IMPACTED
Notropus ludibundus		X	X	//				IMPACTED
Moxostoma congestum			R	PP				IMPACTED
Etheostoma grahami	X	X	X	PP	X			IMPACTED
Cyprinella cf.rutila	X	X	X	//		R		IMPACTED
Notropis amabilis	X	X	X	PP	X	X		IMPACTED
Dionda cf. punctifer	X	X	X	//	X	X		IMPACTED
Dionda diaboli		X	X	EP	X	X		IMPACTED
Lepomis megalotis	X	X	X	//	X	X	X	
Astyanax mexicanus	X	X	X	//	X	X	X	
Cichlasoma cyanoguttatus	X	X	X	//	X	X	X	
Lepomis macrochirus		X		//		X	X	X
Micropterus salmoides		X		//	X	X	X	
Gambusia affinis	X			//	R	R	R	

++ – Species recently extinct due to poor management.

EP – In danger of extinction. This species should be protected by all authorities in the country under Ley de Normatividad, August 2, 1993.

PP – Threatened. These species appear to have a threat of extinction as of May 17, 1991.

LVG, GAG, and SCB = Collections of Luciano Val Guerra, Graciela Arocha Gomez, and Salvador Contreras Balderas.

Invasive species

Hydrilla *(Hydrilla verticillata)* is a non-native macrophyte found in Amistad Reservoir. The major problem associated with this species is the plant's fast growth, which can render the areas where it is found unusable. Hydrilla can clog canals, hinder access to boat docks and make shoreline fishing difficult if not impossible. Problem areas are most often associated with developed to highly developed areas. In Amistad Reservoir, the majority of the shoreline is without development, and the reservoir is deeper than many others. As a result, Hydrilla has not created any problems to date and control measures have not been recommended.

Prymnesium parvum, a species of golden alga, was documented in Texas for the first time in the Pecos River in the 1980's. The alga is toxic to gill breathing organisms, but is not known to harm humans or other species. The alga has not been documented in the reservoir proper.

On the Mexico side of the reservoir there have been no problems with aggressive species, except possibly with the striped bass that was introduced on the United States side of the reservoir. This bass is very aggressive and voracious and potentially represents a negative impact on other aquatic fauna. The striped bass was introduced by the United States but the full extent to the impact on Lake Amistad has not been determined. Many scientific manuscripts have been published which indicate striped bass primarily eat gizzard shad and have little impact on other fish populations in reservoirs (Axton and Whitehurst, 1985; Bettoli et al, 1995; Combs, 1979, 1982; Harper and Namminga, 1986; Jenkins and Morais, 1978; Schramm et al, 1999; Nash et al, 1987).

Status of sport fisheries

Three major sports fisheries are found at Amistad within the US portion of the reservoir- catfish, largemouth bass and striped bass. A catfish fishery, primarily for channel catfish, is very popular. Anglers utilize guide services or may bait areas on their own to aid in location of the fish. The largemouth bass fishery is considered one of the best in the world. The reservoir is very popular with a large number of largemouth bass clubs and tournament directors and consequently receives heavy fishing pressure during the year. The lake record largemouth bass is a 7.13 kilogram (15.68 pound) fish caught in 2005. The third important fishery is for striped bass. The strength and fighting ability of this species have attracted many anglers. Amistad at one time held the State Record for a 20.41 kilogram (45-pound) striped bass.

Under the Federal Aid in Sport Fish Restoration Act, fisheries data has been collected and reported by Texas Parks and Wildlife Department Inland Fisheries Division. Data collected includes standing crop estimates, relative abundance (as determined by catch per unit effort by various sampling techniques), available habitat (structure/vegetation), age and growth rates of major sports fish, creel survey data (April-June 1985) and limited angler access and water quality data. Data and corresponding management plans may be found in Federal Aid in Sport Fish Restoration Act Project F-30-R reports for the following years: 1981,1985, 1986, 1989, 1991, 1993, 1996, and 1999. Starting in 2002, reports will be submitted on a 4-year cycle. Creel surveys to determine directed effort, harvest rates and total angling pressure will be conducted to update the database.

Regulations

Within the Mexico portion of the reservoir, sport fishermen fishing from boats are required to obtain a fishing permit to take fish from Amistad Reservoir. These permits are issued mainly to US citizens who sport fish on Amistad Reservoir. If fishing from the bank, no sport fishing license is required. Table 6 summarizes the number of fishing permits issued by the regional office in Ciudad Acuña from 1995 through 2002.

Table 6. Mexican sport fishing permits issued to anglers fishing from boats in the Amistad Reservoir (Subdelegation of Fishing, Regional Office of Acuña, Coahuila, Mexico

Year	For one Day	Annual	Total	Permits for Boats	Total Number of Permits
1995	1323	156	1479	33	1512
1996	1829	145	1974	26	2000
1997	2320	122	2442	55	2497
1998	2418	120	2538	64	2602
1999	2436	169	2605	72	2677
2000	2420	250	2670	77	2747
2001	2570	270	2840	86	2926
2002	1712	21	1733	8	1741
TOTAL	17028	1253	16548	413	18702

Very little data is available on the amount of recreational harvest from Mexico's side of the reservoir or on the condition of recreational fishery resources.

Within the United States portion of the reservoir, all sport fishermen are required to obtain a Texas fishing license. Since 1998, fishermen operating motorized vessels have also been required to carry a Lake Use Permit. Between 1998 and 2005, the number of annual lake use permits purchased for the US side of the reservoir has ranged between 2,000 and 2,500.

Within Mexico, recreational sport fishing can be done from shore, on board boats or underwater. Whoever conducts this activity from shoreline doesn't need a permit, but must utilize only authorized fishing gear, such as fishing poles or fishing line and hooks, with bait or lures and respect the minimum sizes and limits of capture that is determined by CONAPESCA. Fishing permits are provided individually and are not transferable to others, and corresponding rights of the permit are provided during payment of the permit, as established by SAT (Servicio de Administración Tributaria).

Fish captured through recreational sport fishing are destined for personal consumption or for taxidermy display.

Sport fishing boats can carry on board as many fishing poles desired by fishermen, but the capture of fish made by fishermen must follow the limits and conditions established, namely: 10 fish daily per fisherman, but no more than 5 fish from one species. During fishing trips that are more than three days, the number of fish accumulated per sport fisherman must not exceed the three-day quota.

Prohibitions

- Unauthorized fish species or number of fish species retained.
- Capture crustaceans, mollusks, reptiles and amphibians.
- The use of dragging nets.
- The use of artificial illumination to attract fish.
- Fishing in re-population zones or during closed season.
- The use of fishing lures that include treble hooks.
- Processing of fish (fillet) on board a boat.

Status of commercial fishery

In Amistad Reservoir there are only two registered commercial fishing organizations that have authorization for the capture and sale of the different species of fish, with the exception of the various bass. The commercial product is sold as freshly gutted and filleted; in the case of carp, slices with spines are used for chicharrón and ceviche. According to official records from 1985 through 2000, the average yearly catch has been 234.5 metric tons (258.5 tons), with 322.3 metric tons (355.3 tons) being the highest catch in 1988, and 106.6 metric tons (117.5 tons) being the smallest catch in 2000. The current fishing fleet consists of 27 outboard motor vessels, 319 nets and 28 members (individuals) in the fishing cooperatives.

All the catch is gutted; only the carp and gar are filleted and frozen when their supply is excessive. All the production is sold in northern Coahuila.

Table 7. Fish production registered for Amistad Reservoir and size of the catches according to the arrival notifications submitted by the Mexican fishing cooperatives

Year/Año	Kg/Lbs
1985	158,103 / 348,557
1986	228,373 / 503,476
1987	344,682 / 759,893
1988	322,355 / 710,670
1989	318,210 / 701,532
1990	291,780 / 643,264
1991	291,525 / 642,702
1992	159,468 / 351,566
1993	208,135 / 458,859
1994	216,926 / 478,239
1995	205,937 / 454,013

1996	210,100 / 463,191
1997	235,000 / 518,086
1998	228,025 / 502,708
1999	226,112 / 498,491
2000	106,685 / 235,200
TOTAL	**3,751,416 / 8,270,446**

The share of each of the species in the total population, taking as a reference the catch of one year, is:

Catfish	42.0%
Freshwater Drum	15.0
Carp	10.0
Smallmouth buffalo	<1.0
Gar	<1.0
Tilapia	<1.0
Shad	26.0
Others	+4.0
	100.0%

Catfish – *(Ictalurus punctatus, I.catus, I.furcatus, I.melas.)* Catfish is the most abundant species, representing 42% of all captures. They are primarily caught with highly selective traps that allow for a certain size. The largest proportion of all individuals is between 27 and 47 cm (10.64 and 18.52 in.) standard length, and the average weight is 1kg (2 lbs), with the largest weighing up to 7 kg (15 lbs).

Freshwater Drum – Drum represents an average of 15% of all catch. Drum is caught with gill nets with mesh openings of at least 4 inches. The average size is from 28 to 40 cm (11.03 to 15.76 in) standard length.

Carp – Carp represents about 10% of the total catch and are normally caught with gill nets with various mesh openings of at least 4 inches. Sizes are from 27 to 60 cm (10.64 to 23.64 in) with a large number more than 9 kg (20 lbs). The average weight of this species is 1.5 kg (3 lbs). They are sold as fillets and sliced.

Smallmouth Buffalo – It has been displaced by the catfish because the catfish is more readily accepted in the market.

Gar – Its commercial exploitation had a large potential, but it now has very little acceptance and the costs of catching it are very high.

Tilapia – There is a large demand for this species, but due to water temperature conditions, it has not been possible to establish a productive stock of this fish.

Shad – It is primarily used as bait, though on occasion strips of this fish are used in ceviche.

Mexican fisheries studies

Investigators from the Instituto Nacional de la Pesca Central Regional Fisheries Studies, Patzcuaro completed a fish biology study in Amistad Reservoir during 1997-1998 (Orbe-Mendoza and Hernández-Montaño, 2000). The study objectives were: to evaluate the fishery; to identify the commercial fish species; to determine the fishery pressure on the reservoir and the fishing equipment most appropriate for selectivity; and to analyze the fishery in accordance with the National Fishing Registry. The goal was to propose a strategy for fishing regulations that would produce a sustainable resource.

As a result of the study, the following recommendations and methods for regulating the reservoir's fisheries resources were proposed:

- Plan harvest by using fishing permits.

- Utilize selective fishing methods such as gill nets with mesh openings of 4 inches or greater, with a maximum length of 100 meters (328 feet), and a depth of 2 to 3 meters (6.6 to 9.8 feet), for the harvest of tilapia, carp, drum, catfish, and gar. Utilize traps for the harvest of carp and catfish with the minimal determined size, rejecting smaller individuals.

- Harvesting species with the following minimal size limits:
  - Catfish   32 cm (12.6 in) (all species)
  - Drum   29 cm (11.4 in)
  - Carp   30 cm (11.8 in)
  - Bass *(Lobina)* 34 cm (13.4 in) (white)
  - Bass *(Róbalo)* 38 cm (15.0 in) (green and striped)
  - Flathead   45 cm (17.7 in)
  - Crappie   26 cm (10.2 in)
  - Bluegill   15 cm (5.9 in) (redear sunfish and bluegill)

- Allow a fishing force of 40 fishermen with 8 nets per fisherman.

- Lay nets from Buoy 8 to the uppermost point of the lake from 6pm on Sunday until retrieval by 8pm on Friday. Nets must be checked once every 24 hours.

- Continue with stocking of commercial and sport fishes.

- Undertake taxonomic and biological studies of the fishes, along with ecological studies to fully understand the ecosystem.

- Improve the harvest registry.

- Train the fishermen in various subjects such as fishing methods; processing fish and their sale, in order to increase the value of the fish, and tourist services, etc.

- Promote the advancement of sport fishing that will increase fishermen's income.

- Utilize Norma Oficial Mexicana NOM-017-Pesc-1994, to regulate sport fishing activities in the waters under the jurisdiction of Mexico.

- Undertake a socioeconomic fishery study.

- Establish an official Mexican law to regulate the development of the fisheries resources of Amistad Reservoir.

Habitat limitations

Amistad Reservoir experiences dramatic water level fluctuations and on August 5, 1998, the reservoir was more than 58 vertical feet (17.7 meters) below conservation pool level (see Figure 2 for historic water surface elevation for Amistad Reservoir). From 1992 through 2002, the reservoir fluctuated at approximately 25% of capacity due to a regional drought.

Spawning success of nest building centrachids, including largemouth bass, may be enhanced by stable conditions during the spawning season. Downstream water demand and reservoir drawdown during the spring spawning period may impact year class production.

Spawning success of free spawners, such as striped bass and white bass, may be enhanced by rising water levels when there is adequate flow into the reservoir. Periods of drought, low lake levels, and low flows may negatively impact the spawning success of these fish.

Given that many fish of commercial and recreational importance may be affected when CILA and IBWC increase water releases for downstream needs in the spring, adjustments in the timing and duration of water releases may enhance spawning success of recreationally and economically important species in Amistad Reservoir.

Figure 2. IBWC water surface elevation for Amistad Reservoir

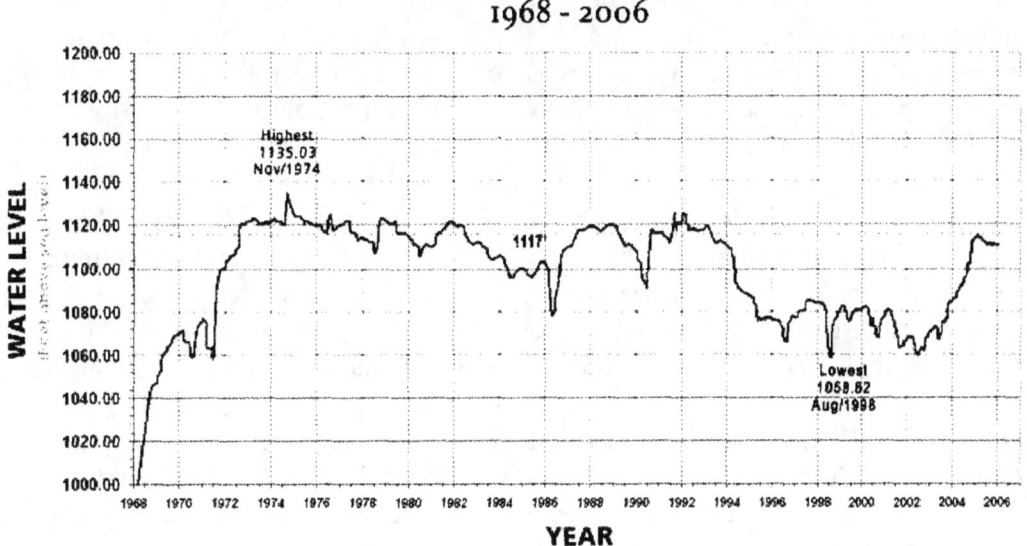

AMISTAD RESERVOIR LEVEL
1968 - 2006

MAJOR ISSUES OF CONCERN

Recreational - commercial fisheries conflicts

Currently, there are two differing goals of fisheries management in effect for the US and Mexico at Amistad Reservoir. The TPWD and NPS are charged with monitoring, protection, and improvement of the sports fishery. All management and stocking programs presently conducted by these two agencies are aimed at the sports fishery. The major sport species include largemouth bass, channel catfish, blue catfish, striped bass, smallmouth bass and white crappie.

Conversely, while Mexico actively manages for enhanced sport fishing of black bass through stockings and regulations, the goals also target monitoring and protecting the commercial fishery. Currently, certain species found in Amistad are subject to commercial harvest. Non-designated species for commercial harvest will not be commercially sold. See Table 3 for commercial, sport, and commercial/sport species.

There is a perception that the removal of species such as carp, buffalo, carp suckers and tilapia by commercial netting may actually benefit the sports fishery found at Amistad. Conversely, the removal of species considered sports fish by netting activities is perceived to adversely impact the overall sports fishery found in Amistad. No scientific data is available to substantiate either of these views. Catfish represent the primary fish of recreational and commercial conflict, as this species comprises a large portion of both the US recreational and Mexico commercial harvest.

Increasing recreational use and tournaments

The United States side of the reservoir has experienced a significant increase in organized fishing tournaments since the mid 1980's. Existing visitor use facilities at Amistad NRA were not designed to accommodate large fishing tournaments. Developing guidance and management of tournament impacts within the context of existing or new facility development is needed.

Amistad averaged about 20 bass fishing tournaments a year in the 1980's, which has increased to around 150 tournaments a year, including many championship tournaments. Some large tournaments involve as many as 250 boats. Neither the United States side nor the Mexico side of the reservoir currently has adequate facilities to accommodate these large tournaments, which are vital to the local economy. Existing parking areas and launch ramps overfill during large tournaments, resulting in negative impacts to the visitor experience. Development of a facility for tournaments to weigh-in their fish is also needed. Organizers using the Diablo East boat ramp on the United States side currently provide temporary weigh-in facilities in a parking lot, requiring contestants to bring their boats out of the water, transfer their fish to plastic bags, then release the fish down a 200 ft. (70 m) tube back to the water. A mortality study conducted during an August 1998 tournament estimated that 65% of the 2400 fish caught during the tournament died after being released (Wilde et al, 2002). Many bass tournament

---

organizers, and local, State, Federal and Mexican officials, are interested in reducing fish mortality during these tournaments.

Within Mexico, sport fishing, as authorized by SAGARPA, is conducted by fishermen from both countries. The species preferred by the sport fishermen are black bass and striped bass. However, this activity has been marginally practiced due to the lack of infrastructure. This problem requires that the state tourism agency, Instituto Estatal de Turismo, and the Department of Communications and Transportation, Secretaría de Comunicaciones y Transportes, coordinate their efforts. It is also necessary that Mexican sport fishermen go through some training to learn how to fish in tournaments and how to manage and promote tournaments and be more active in the management and promotions of tournaments, for this activity is also a good source of income in the northern region of the state of Coahuila.

Despite these difficulties, in recent years sport fishing in Mexico has undergone a solid expansion. This is shown by the number of permits issued by the regional office in Ciudad Acuña, which increased from 1,479 in 1995 to 2,670 in 2000. The increase includes both daily and monthly fishing permits (See Table 6).

In the state of Coahuila there are close to 20 hunting, shooting and fishing clubs. Additionally there are social organizations like the Lions and the Rotary Clubs, all of which organize fishing tournaments. It is the right of the sub-delegation of fishing, Subdelegación de Pesca, to regulate and control fishing tournaments, in order to contribute to recreation and leisure of the population within the state. On the Mexico side of Amistad Reservoir, approximately 10 tournaments per year took place from 1995-2000, consisting of approximately 70 participants each.

The present practice of "Catch and Release" and its increasing popularity have probably reduced overall harvest by anglers. Creel surveys should be conducted to determine the current level of harvest. Data from tournaments held for largemouth bass should be collected to allow catch rates to be monitored. Trend data will allow the determination of increases or decreases.

Delayed mortality from catch and release tournaments may present a potential problem. Seasonal adjustments should be made in scheduling tournaments to avoid periods of high water and air temperatures. High delayed mortality has been documented from tournaments held during the summer. As a alternative to "Catch/Hold and Release" tournaments, paper (recorded length and/or photo) tournaments should be considered during the summer season.

Fishing access

The fishing access on the United States side of the reservoir is considered very good; however, the access on the Mexico side of the reservoir is limited to one high-water ramp located at Playa Tlaloc. This site provides the only current public access to the reservoir. The State of Coahuila has considered constructing an additional ramp; however, the northwest section of the reservoir on the Mexico side is almost entirely surrounded by private property, which greatly limits potential locations for expanded public access.

Record drought conditions from 1992-2002 resulted in a significant downturn in the reservoir water level, resulting in major disruptions to visitor use facilities. Most of the boat launch ramps on the United States side of the reservoir were inoperable in 2001. In August of 1998, when Amistad Reservoir reached its historic low water level of 1058.62', as few as 2 of the 17 developed launch ramps were in use. The Pecos River launch ramp, the only launch ramp on the western end of the reservoir, didn't return to operation until the water level increased to 1086' in March of 2004.

IBWC has advised that the reservoir may rarely, if ever, maintain a full conservation pool level. Visitor complaints and dissatisfaction about the closure of high-water facilities, and lack of access at low water levels, is expected to remain an issue.

Water quality/quantity/regulation

The issue of water quality is secondary to water quantity at this time. Low flows entering the reservoir and a rapidly declining water level (during fish spawning seasons) negatively impact fish spawning and recruitment.

It is recommended that one goal for water managers is to maintain a stable water level for a period of 2 months after the major spawning season for largemouth bass.

Conflicting use

Other than perceived problems between sports fishermen and commercial fishermen, the possibility of conflict between personal watercraft (jet skis), ski boats and anglers could arise. However, at current use levels, conflicts do not seem to exist. Because of the size of Amistad, it is felt any such conflict could be easily resolved through the implementation of specific-use zones.

Education and outreach

The public holds numerous misperceptions about the fisheries and conditions at Amistad. Examples include Mexico fishing license requirements, impacts of the commercial fishing cooperatives, and tournament effects on the black bass population. There is a general need for better public education concerning fisheries management.

The final approved Binational Fisheries Management Plan should be presented to interested parties in Del Rio and in Ciudad Acuña. Bulletin boards at major access points should be utilized to promote the management plan. In addition, public scoping meetings will be mandated when any new regulation proposal is made, and communication between the US and Mexico should continue.

Within Mexico, sport fishermen want to improve the fishing potential of this resource. They also want sustainable development of the fishing resources of the reservoir. There is, however, a need for more promotional efforts on the part of the sub-delegation of fishing, *Subdelegación de Pesca*. This agency needs to provide more information about minimum sizes and maximum number of specimens that can be harvested. The sub-delegation also has to facilitate the process of obtaining permits; especially for the American fishermen who come during the weekend, when its offices are closed. The agency should also communicate the need for more tourist infrastructure for the proper development of sport fishing in Mexico.

Additionally, the sub-delegation agency should use the media to promote recreational fishing and inform the public of prohibited activities and the requirements to practice this sport. Finally, the agency should install signs that adequately show how to access the reservoir.

COOPERATIVE MANAGEMENT PROGRAM

Management goals

All parties to this Binational Fisheries Management Plan agree to the following common goals and objectives in carrying out a cooperative effort in the management of the fishery resources of Amistad Reservoir. Tasks which are necessary to achieve our common goals and objectives are identified and will be carried out by the parties indicated to fulfill this cooperative endeavor.

Goal 1: Establish a lasting working relationship between United States, State of Texas, and Mexico managers with responsibility for fisheries and aquatic resources in Lake Amistad.

> **Objective:** Establish a binational management program based on a Fisheries Management Plan that will provide future conservation managers with guidelines and agreements for the management of the recreation, fisheries, and aquaculture found at Amistad Reservoir.

> > **Task:** Complete a Binational Fisheries Management Plan and further develop a binational management program of communication and cooperation (Texas Parks and Wildlife Department, National Park Service, US Fish and Wildlife Service, Secretaria de Agricultura, Ganaderia, Desarrollo Rural, Pesca y Alimentacion; Commision Nacional de Pesca; Secretaria de Fomento Agropecuario e Instiuto Estatal de Turismo del Gobierno del Estado; Instituto Nacional de la Pesca; Comision Nacional del Agua; Secretaria de Comunicaciones y Transportes).

> > **Task:** Review the Binational Plan, modify as necessary, and renew agreements for continued binational cooperation at 5 year intervals (all signing agencies).

> > **Task:** Improve the coordination and data sharing of water quality monitoring activities on Amistad Reservoir (SAGARPA, CILA, CNA, TCEQ, IBWC, TPWD, USGS).

> **Objective:** Ensure that efforts to implement the Binational Fisheries Management Plan are coordinated.

> > **Task:** Signatories (or representative of signatories) of the plan meet at least once a year to discuss progress toward management goals and coordinate planned activities. The agencies may meet more frequently if necessary (all signing agencies).

> > **Task:** In addition, these agencies agree to inform each other of all management actions that potentially have an effect on reservoir fisheries (e.g., stocking species, changing harvest regulations, or initiating new fisheries activities) prior to implementation. See Appendix II for agency contacts.

Goal 2: Coordinate with the Secretary of Communication and Transport and the Central SCT of Coahuila.

Objective: Provide assistance with communication and equipment that is used in that sector (telephones, mail, etc.).

Objective: Provide assistance with transportation infrastructure and materials. Through coordination with the state government and the municipality, facilitate maintenance and upgrades to the network of roads and boat ramps that access Amistad Reservoir.

In reference to the above objective, advice will be given when needed on:
Boat launching, operation and associated rules.

Goal 3: Manage the fisheries of Amistad Reservoir in a manner that would benefit both sport and commercial fishermen.

Objective: Maintain and enhance, where possible, catch rates and quality of recreational sport fishing for the following species:

Largemouth Bass (*Micropterus salmoides)*
Smallmouth Bass *(Micropterus dolomieu*)
Spotted Bass *(Micropterus punctulatus*)
Striped Bass *(Morone saxatilis*)
White Bass *(Morone chrysops*)
White Crappie *(Pomoxis annularis*)
Channel Catfish *(Ictalurus punctatus*)
Blue Catfish (Rio Grande strain) *(Ictalurus furcatus* spp.)
Flathead Catfish *(Pylodictis olivaris*)

Task: Monitor status of fish species through scientific fish population surveys and make efforts to standardize sampling operations between US, Texas and Mexico, and whenever possible, to improve the quality and quantity of fish population data (TPWD, SAGARPA, Subdelegacion de Pesca, State of Coahuila, NPS).

Task: Stock as necessary to maintain healthy populations and enhance the fishery (TPWD, SAGARPA, NPS). Note: Texas will stock fish when TPWD criteria are met, and Mexico will stock by their criteria. However, both agree to seek input from each other on the development of stocking plans and to notify each other when stocking actions occur. All agencies agree to prohibit unapproved private stocking of fish into Amistad Reservoir. No private stocking is allowed unless sanctioned by agency. Stocking criteria for TPWD are provided in Appendix V.

Task: Monitor harvest by sports anglers (TPWD, NPS, SAGARPA, State of Coahuila).

Task: Establish a common form for recording fishing tournament catches (TPWD, NPS, SAGARPA, State of Coahuila).

Task: Reduce sport fishing tournament mortality by providing improved management facilities and protocols (NPS, TPWD, SAGARPA, State of Coahuila).

Task: Modify harvest regulations as necessary to maintain healthy sustainable fisheries and to achieve management objectives (TPWD, SAGARPA, NPS).

Task: Share all information and data on the status and condition of the sports fishery (NPS, TPWD, SAGARPA, INP, State of Coahuila). See Appendix II for contact information.

Objective: Maintain a healthy sustainable commercial fishery which supports the current number of commercial fishermen for the following species:

Aplondinotus grunniens   *Carpoides carpio*
Catostomus comersonni   *Ictiobus prinellus*
Cyprinus carpio   *Dorosoma cepedianum*
Tilapis ssp   *Noemigonus crysoleucas*
Ictalurus furcatus   *Pimephales promelas*
Ictalurus catus   *Lipisosteus osseus*
Ameiurus melas   *Lipisosteus oculatus*
Ameiurus nebulosas   *Lepomis macrochirus*
Ictalurus punctatus   *Lepomis microlopus*
Pylodictis olivaris

Task: Monitor harvest by commercial fishermen (SAGARPA and State of Coahuila).

Task: Stock these commercially harvested species as necessary to maintain fishery stocks. The introduction of any other species will require the prior approval of all signatories to this agreement.

Task: Share commercial harvest information with all signatories to the agreement (SAGARPA and State of Coahuila). See Appendix II for agency contacts.

Goal 4: Document the economic value of the Amistad Reservoir recreational and commercial fishery and measure angler satisfaction with the recreational fishery.

Objective: Assign economic values to all aspects of the fishery on Amistad Reservoir.

    Task: Design and conduct a cooperative economic study (TPWD, NPS, SAGARPA).

Objective: Determine angler use/attitudes.

    Task: Conduct a creel survey to determine current angler usage and collect names and addresses for a follow-up economic study (NPS, TPWD, SAGARPA).

Goal 5: Maintain the overall health and viable populations of native and endemic fish species that occur within the localized watershed of Amistad Reservoir.

Objective: Protect native fish populations found in Amistad Reservoir and within the immediate watershed.

    Task: Conduct fish inventories on the Rio Grande, Pecos, and Devils Rivers to determine presence and current population status of native fish species. These surveys would occur at locations determined by all participating agencies. (TPWD, SAGARPA, USFWS, NPS).

Objective: Promote native fish populations found in Amistad Reservoir.

    Task: As a recognized protocol, stock when feasible, native fish in the Amistad Reservoir for sport and commercial uses. (TPWD, SAGARPA).

    Task: Control the introduction of fish species to the Amistad Reservoir and local watershed that are not on the above list of desired species (see Goal 3). Follow specific agency criteria when stocking non-specified species for sport and commercial use (TPWD, SAGARPA, NPS, USFWS). See Appendices IV and V.

Goal 6: Maintain or improve sport fishing access to Amistad Reservoir.

Objective: Ensure that Amistad Reservoir remains accessible for sport fishing at all water levels.

    Task: Plan for the development of one permanent low-water boat ramp for the Mexico side of the reservoir (SAGARPA, CILA).

Goal 7: Improve angler understanding of fishing regulations, fees, and license requirements for Amistad Reservoir in both Mexico and the United States.

Objective: Create educational information for anglers that describes procedures required for fishing on Amistad Reservoir.

> **Task:** Develop a common informational fact sheet on boat access, fees, facilities available, and basic fishing regulations.

> **Task:** Develop a common web-page and links for public information about the reservoir and its recreational opportunities.

Management protocols

Regulation changes
Individual agency protocols for implementing new management regulations are presented in Appendix VI.

Implementation of the Binational Management Plan committee
The plan will be reviewed for necessary modifications by all signatories at 5-year intervals. Suggested changes will be provided in writing to the other agencies and be discussed at the annual meeting of signatories. Formal changes will require the signatures of all participants to constitute an amendment to the plan.

Annual meetings will be held during the first week of August. Meetings will be held in Ciudad Acuña and Del Rio on an annually rotating basis. The annual meeting will involve a joint evaluation of the program to date, a review of accomplishments of the previous year, a discussion of agency proposals and planned actions for the upcoming year, and a discussion of general points of agreement on necessary management actions.

Each country will name a principal person of contact for sharing of data information. See Appendix II for current contact list for SAGARPA, TPWD, and NPS.

Management constraints
The signatories agree to carry out the provisions of this Binational Agreement to the extent that their respective administrative funding will permit.

All parties agree that nothing in this agreement is considered to supersede their legal mandates and agency governing policies.

PUBLIC INVOLVEMENT AND ENVIRONMENTAL IMPACT REVIEW

The signatory agencies have determined that this plan is categorically excluded from environmental impact review under the US National Environmental Policy Act (NEPA) and the Environmental Policy Act of the State of Texas, as it does not propose specific new management actions. The completed plan will be made available to the public.

Implementation of specific projects or management actions that may be developed or proposed as a result of this plan will require full compliance with the above Acts, Mexico's environmental review process, and/or all other federal environmental initiatives and policies. This compliance might range from additional categorical exclusions to a full Environmental Impact Statement, depending on the magnitude of the project and public interest. Projects within the reservoir may require Corps of Engineer (COE) permits. NEPA actions and COE permits will require public review and comment. The necessary permits and environmental compliance will be acquired during project planning and development.

LITERATURE CITED

Axon, J. R. and D. K. Whitehurst. 1985. Striped bass management in lakes with emphasis on management problems. Trans. Am. Fish. Soc. 114:8-11.

Bettoli, P.W., R. Osborne, and S. Owens. 1995. A review of the literature pertaining to the effects of striped bass on other fish populations. Final Rep. Tenn. Coop. Fish Res. Unit, Cookville, Tenn. 10pp.

Combs, D. L. 1979. Food habits of adult striped bass from Keystone Reservoir and its tail waters. Proc. Annu. Conf. Southeast. Assoc. Fish and Wild. Agencies. 32:571-575.

Combs, D. L. 1982. Fish population changes in Keystone Reservoir fourteen years after striped bass introductions. Proc. Annu. Conf. Southeast. Assoc. Fish and Wild. Agencies. 34:167-174.

Harper, J. L. and H. E. Namminga. 1986. Fish population trends in Texoma Reservoir following establishment of striped bass. Pages 156-165 in G. E. Hall and M. J. Van Den Avyle, eds. Reservoir fisheries management: strategies for the 1980's. Am. Fish. Soc. South. Div., Res. Comm. Bethesda, Md.

Jenkins, R. M. and D. J. Morais. 1978. Prey-predator relations in predator-stocking-evaluation reservoirs. Proc. Annu. Conf. Southeast. Assoc. Fish and Wild. Agencies. 30:141-157.

Kurzawski, Ken. 2001. A bass act. Texas Parks and Wildlife Magazine. 59(1): 24-29. Austin, Texas.

Nash, V. E., W. E. Hayes, R. L. Self and J. P. Kirk. 1987. Effects of striped bass introduction in Lake Watertree, South Carolina. Proc. Annu. Conf. Southeast. Assoc. Fish and Wild. Agencies. 41:48-54.

Orbe-Mendoza, A. A. and D. Hernández-Montaño. 2000. Evaluación Biológico-Pesquera de la Presa La Amistad, Coahuila, Méx. – Texas, E.U. Informe Técnico. Instituto Nacional de la Pesca. México. 25 pp.

Schramm, H. L., J. E. Kraai, and C. R. Munger. 2001. Intensive stocking of striped bass to restructure a gizzard shad population in a eutrophic Texas reservoir. Proc. Annu. Conf. Southeast. Assoc. Fish and Wild. Agencies. 53:180-192.

Texas Natural Heritage Program. 1995. Biological Survey of Lake Amistad Recreation Site. Texas Parks and Wildlife Department. Resource Protection Division. Austin, Texas.

Water Resources Scoping Report. 2001. Technical Report NPS/NRWRD/NRTR-2001/295. Amistad National Recreation Area. National Park Service. Department of the Interior.

Wilde, G.R., D.H. Larson, W.H. Redell and G.R. Wilde III. 2002. Mortality of Black Bass Captured in Three Fishing Tournaments on Lake Amistad, Texas. Texas J. Sci. 54(2):125-132.

PROJECT NEEDS

The signatory Agencies have identified the following projects as current high priority studies and actions that need to be taken to improve knowledge and/or management of the fishery resources within Amistad Reservoir. Appendix VII contains more detailed descriptions for each of the 12 potential projects listed below.

1) Determine total economic value of fisheries and angler use and attitudes at the Amistad Reservoir (INP, SAGARPA, TPWD, NPS).

2) Determine the level of total sport fish harvest occurring on the reservoir (TPWD, SAGARPA, NPS).

3) Conduct cooperative monitoring (studies) of commercial and sport fish populations (TPWD, INP, SAGARPA, NPS).

4) Develop sport fishing tournament weigh-in facilities that result in reduced mortality (NPS, TPWD, SAGARPA, State of Coahuila, Institute of Tourism).

5) Improve reservoir access (roads and boat ramps) on both sides of the reservoir (NPS, Secretaria de Comunicaciones y Transporte, Instituto estatal de Turismo).

6) Develop a common informational fact sheet on boat access, fishing fees, facilities available, basic regulations, etc. (TPWD, NPS, SAGARPA).

7) Establish a common form for recording fishing tournament catches (TPWD, NPS, SAGARPA).

8) Develop a common web page and links for public information about the reservoir and its recreational opportunities (TPWD, NPS, SAGARPA).

9) Improve the coordination of water quality monitoring activities on the reservoir (NPS, TCEQ, TPWD, CNA).

10) Evaluate contamination sources and issues (TCEQ, NPS,CNA).

11) Determine the actual state of long-term institutional monitoring (TPWD, NPS, SAGARPA).

12) Conduct experimental studies about the effects of commercial fishing nets on sport fishes.

APPENDICES

Appendix I. Checklist of fish present in Amistad Reservoir

Reported by Texas Parks and Wildlife Department

Scientific name	Common name	Occurrence
Lepisosteus oculatus	Spotted gar	Present
Lepisosteus osseus	Longnose gar	Present
Lepisosteus spatula	Alligator gar	Present
Dorosoma cepedianum	Gizzard shad	Abundant
Dorosoma petenense	Threadfin shad	Abundant
Carassius auratus	Goldfish	Rare
Cyprinella lutrensis	red shiner	Abundant
Cyprinella proserpina	proserpine shiner	Present
Cyprinella venusta	blacktail shiner	Abundant
Cyprinus carpio	common carp	Abundant
Dionda argentosa	manantial roundnose minnow	Abundant
Dionda diaboli	Devils River minnow	Rare
Dionda episcopa	roundnose minnow	Present
Macrhybopsis aestivalis	speckled chub	Rare
Notemigonus crysoleucas	golden shiner	Present
Notropis amabilis	Texas shiner	Abundant
Notropis braytoni	Tamaulipas shiner	Abundant
Notropis chihuahua	Chihuahua shiner	Rare
Notropis jemezanus	Rio Grande shiner	Rare
Notropis stramineus	sand shiner	Abundant
Pimephales vigilax	bullhead minnow	Abundant
Rhinichthys cataractae	longnose dace	Rare
Carpiodes carpio	river carpsucker	Abundant
Cycleptus elongatus	blue sucker	Rare
Ictiobus bubalus	smallmouth buffalo	Abundant
Moxostoma austrinum	west Mexican redhorse	Rare
Moxostoma congestum	gray redhorse	Abundant
Astyanax mexicanus	Mexican tetra	Abundant
Ameiurus natalis	yellow bullhead	Present
Ictalurus furcatus	blue catfish	Present
Ictalurus lupus	headwater catfish	Rare
Ictalurus punctatus	channel catfish	Abundant
Noturus gyrinus	tadpole madtom	Rare
Pylodictis olivaris	flathead catfish	Abundant
Cyprinodon eximius	Conchos pupfish	Rare
Cyprinodon hybrids	sheepshead minnow x Pecos pupfish	Rare
Fundulus grandis	Gulf killifish	Present
Gambusia affinis	western mosquitofish	Present
Gambusia geiseri	largespring gambusia	Present
Gambusia senilis	blotched gambusia	Extirpated
Gambusia speciosa	Mexican mosquitofish	Abundant
Poecilia latipinna	sailfin molly	Present
Menidia beryllina	inland silverside	Abundant

Morone chrysops	white bass	Abundant
Morone saxatilis	striped bass	Abundant
Lepomis auritus	redbreast sunfish	Abundant
Lepomis cyanellus	green sunfish	Abundant
Lepomis gulosus	warmouth	Abundant
Lepomis macrochirus	bluegill	Abundant
Lepomis megalotis	longear sunfish	Present
Lepomis microlophus	redear sunfish	Present
Micropterus dolomieu	smallmouth bass	Present
Micropterus salmoides	largemouth bass	Abundant
Pomoxis annularis	white crappie	Present
Etheostoma grahami	Rio Grande darter	Present
Percina caprodes	logperch	Abundant
Stizostedion vitreum	walleye	Rare
Aplodinotus grunniens	freshwater drum	Present
Cichlasoma cyanoguttatum	Rio Grande cichlid	Present
Oreochromis aureus	blue tilapia	Present

Reported by SAGARPA Mexico

Ictalurus catus	White catfish
Ictalurus melas	Black bullhead catfish
Ictalurus nebulosus	Brown bullhead catfish
Micropterus punctulatus	Spotted bass
Pomokis nigromaculatus	Black Crappie
Catostomus comersonni	White Sucker
Ictiobus cyprinellus	Bigmouth buffalo
Pimephales promelas	Flathead minnow

Appendix II. Agency contacts

Agency personnel responsible for maintaining the communication network and in charge of informing working group partners on annual meeting dates and new management actions for the Amistad Reservoir fishery will be the following:

1. Subdelegate of Fisheries. SAGARPA, Saltillo, Coahuila, Mexico.
   2003-2005 Contact: Ing. Severo Flores Aguilar.
   Phone (8)44 413-09-12 and 413-05-78.
   E-mail: pesca@coa.sagarpa.gob.mx; acuacultura@coa.sagarpa.gob.mx

2. District Inland Supervisor. TPWD, San Antonio, TX, USA.
   2003-2005 Contact: Randy Myers
   Phone: 210-348-6355.
   E-mail: randy.myers@tpwd.state.tx.us

3. Chief of Resources Management. NPS, Del Rio, TX, USA.
   2003-2005 Contact: Rick Slade.
   Phone: 830-775-7491, ext. 204.
   E-mail: rick_slade@nps.gov

Appendix III. Agency organizational charts

SAGARPA

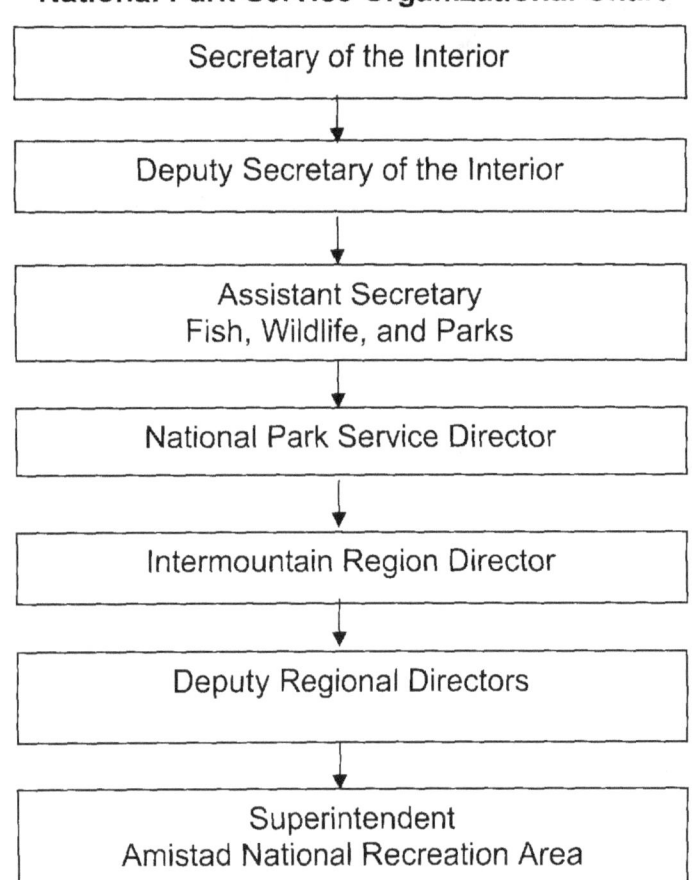

```
┌─────────────────────────────────────────┐
│  SECRETARY OF AGRICULTURE,               │
│  LIVESTOCK, RURAL DEVELOPMENT,           │
│  FISHING AND NUTRITION                   │
└─────────────────────────────────────────┘
        │
   ┌────┴─────────────────┐
   ▼                      ▼
┌──────────────┐   ┌──────────────────┐
│ FISHERIES    │   │ NATIONAL FISHERIES│
│ SUBSECRETARY │   │ INSTITUTE         │
└──────────────┘   └──────────────────┘
   │
   ▼
┌──────────────┐
│ FISHERIES    │
│ MANAGEMENT   │
│ AGENCY       │
└──────────────┘
```

National Park Service Organizational Chart

Secretary of the Interior
Deputy Secretary of the Interior
Assistant Secretary Fish, Wildlife, and Parks
National Park Service Director
Intermountain Region Director
Deputy Regional Directors
Superintendent Amistad National Recreation Area

Texas Parks and Wildlife Department Organizational Chart for Fisheries Management at Amistad Reservoir

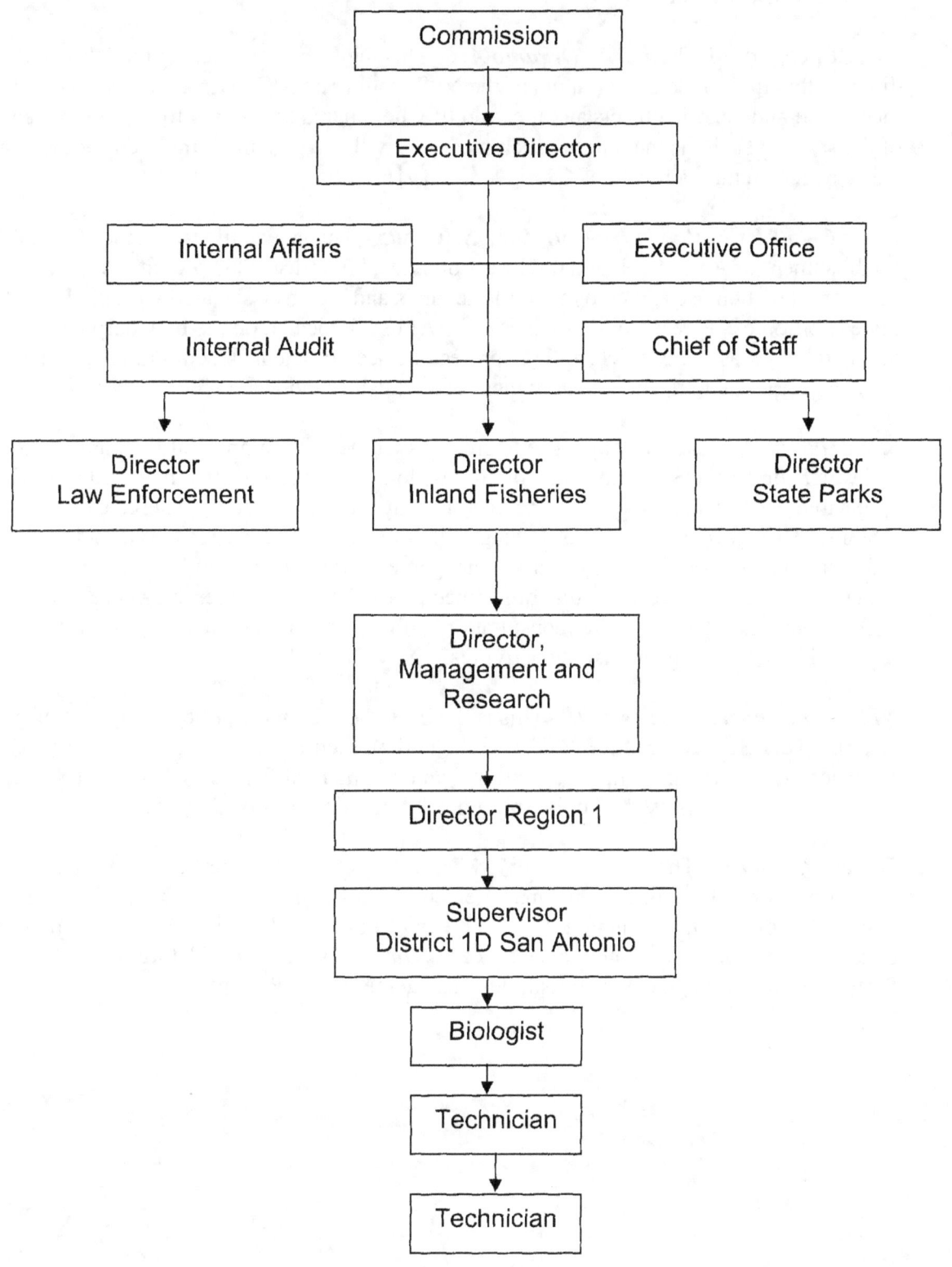

Appendix IV. Overview of management authorities and policies
United States
National Park Service

16 USC, Chapter 1, Section 1. Organic Act - This legislative act created the NPS and directed that the mandate of all units of the NPS would be to "Conserve the scenery and the natural and historic objects and the wild life therein and to provide for the enjoyment of the same in such manner and by such means as will leave them unimpaired for the enjoyment of future generations." August 25, 1916.

16 USC-460-FFF. Public Law 101-628, SEC. 505 - This legislative act authorized the establishment of Amistad National Recreation Area, "In order to (1) provide for public outdoor recreation use and enjoyment of the lands and waters associated with the United States portion of the reservoir known as Lake Amistad, located on the boundary between the State of Texas and Mexico, and (2) protect the scenic, scientific, cultural, and other value contributing to the public enjoyment of such lands and waters."

SEC. 506(d)(1) of the act states "The Secretary shall permit hunting and fishing on lands and waters under the Secretary's jurisdiction within the recreation area in accordance with applicable Federal and State law. The Secretary may designate zones where, and establish periods when, hunting or fishing will not be permitted for reasons of public safety, administration, fish and wildlife management, or public use and enjoyment." (2) "Except in emergencies any regulations issued by the Secretary under this subsection shall be put into effect only after consultation with the appropriate State agencies responsible for hunting and fishing activities." Nov. 28, 1990.

NPS Management Policies 2001 - This is the basic Service-wide policy document of the National Park Service. Chapter 8 (Use of the Parks), section 8.2.2.5 (Fishing) provides guidance on the management of recreational and commercial fishing. Chapter 4 (Harvest of Plants and Animals by the Public) provides information on stocking of fish.

Director's Orders - There are currently 94 Director's Orders that further specify how the NPS policies will be applied to the management of parks and park resources. Director's Order 12 (Conservation Planning, Environmental Impact Analysis, and Decision Making) covers the environmental compliance process. Director's Order 77 (Natural Resource Protection) provides guidance in fisheries management for NPS units.

Amistad NRA General Management Plan (Development Concept Plan) - April 27, 1987
- Management objectives are described in the plan. For resource management, the plan states that the management objectives are to "Protect the quality of water in the lake from internal and external pollution threats," "Maintain a high quality fishery," and under cooperation, "Integrate activities with other agencies sharing responsibility for reservoir and/or recreation area management." Also included under cooperation is the desire to "Continue liaison and cooperation with the government of Mexico." Amistad NRA is scheduled to finalize a new GMP in fiscal year 2007.

Amistad NRA Resources Management Plan - The Resources Management Plan for Amistad NRA was approved in August of 1998. Twenty-eight natural resource project statements are included in this document. AMIS-N-058.001 references the Fisheries Management Plan project.

Strategic Plan - Fiscal Years 2001-2005. This plan was developed from the requirements of the Government Performance and Results Act, 1993. The Strategic Plan contains the following mission goals:
- Goal Category I – Preserve Amistad National Recreation Area's Resources. Two mission goals are included under this category.
  - Mission goal Ia: Natural and cultural resources and associated values are protected, restored, and maintained in good condition and managed within their broader ecosystem and cultural context.
  - Mission goal Ib: The National Park Service contributes to knowledge about natural and cultural resources and associated values; management decisions about resources and visitors are based on adequate scholarly and scientific information.
- Goal Category II – Provide for the public use and enjoyment and visitor experience of Amistad National Recreation Area. Two mission goals are included under this category.
  - Mission goal IIa: Visitors safely enjoy and are satisfied with the availability, accessibility, diversity, and quality of park facilities, services, and appropriate recreational opportunities.
  - Mission goal IIb: Park visitors and the general public understand and appreciate the preservation of the park and its resources for this and future generations.
- Goal Category III – Strengthen and preserve natural and cultural resources and enhance recreational opportunities.

Fishing Tournament Policy - Fishing tournaments are considered special park uses by the NPS and are governed by the following Amistad NRA policy: "As with any special park use, a permit must be requested in advance to allow the park superintendent to confirm that the tournament follows the appropriate laws, is within the values and purposes for which the park was established, that public safety is paramount, that the property and resources are protected, and that normal activities and operations of the park can be continued." A special use permit is required when any fishing tournament exceeds ten boats.

36 CFR Part 2.3 (Fishing) provides the following general guidance: "Except in designated areas or as provided in this section, fishing shall be in accordance with the laws and regulations of the State within whose exterior boundaries a park or portion thereof is located." 36 CRR Part 2.3(d)(4) prohibits "Commercial fishing, except where specifically authorized by Federal statutory law."

36 CFR Part 7.79 is a special regulation for Amistad National Recreation Area that includes the following language in Subpart b: "Unless otherwise designated, fishing in a manner authorized under applicable State law is allowed". April 16, 1969.

Superintendent's Compendium to 36 CFR - In accordance with 36 CFR Part 1.7(b), the compendium establishes designations, closures, permit requirements and other restrictions under the discretionary authority of the Superintendent of Amistad National Recreation Area. The compendium identifies fishing under section 2.3. This section provides closure notices for certain areas of the reservoir. Under section 2.14, disposing of fish remains is covered along with the designation of fish cleaning stations.

US Fish & Wildlife Service

Policy for Conserving Species Listed or Proposed for Listing Under the Endangered Species Act While Providing and Enhancing Recreational Fisheries Opportunities - This policy address the conservation needs of species listed, or proposed to be listed, under the Endangered Species Act (ESA) while providing for the continuation and enhancement of recreational fisheries. This policy identifies measures the Service will take to ensure consistency in the administration of the ESA, promote collaboration with other Federal, State, and Tribal fisheries managers, and improve and increase efforts to inform nonfederal entities of the requirements of the ESA while enhancing recreational fisheries. June 3, 1996.

16 U.S.C. 742a-742j – The Fish and Wildlife Act of August 8, 1956, as frequently amended, establishes a comprehensive national fish, shellfish, and wildlife resources policy with emphasis on the commercial fishing industry but also with a direction to administer the Act with regard to the inherent right of every citizen and resident to fish for pleasure, enjoyment, and betterment and to maintain and increase public opportunities for recreational use of fish and wildlife resources.

16 U.S.C. 661-667e – The Fish and Wildlife Coordination Act of 1934, as frequently amended, authorizes the Secretaries of Agriculture and Commerce to provide assistance to and cooperate with Federal and State agencies to protect, rear, stock, and increase the supply of game and fur-bearing animals. The Act also authorizes the Fish and Wildlife Service to prepare plans to protect wildlife resources, the completion of wildlife surveys on public lands, and requires consultation with the Fish and Wildlife Service where the "waters of any stream or other body of water are proposed or authorized, permitted or licensed to be impounded, diverted . . . or otherwise controlled or modified" by any agency under a Federal permit or license.

16 U.S.C. 1531-1544 – Endangered Species Act of 1973, as amended, provides for the conservation of ecosystems upon which threatened and endangered species of fish, wildlife, and plants depend, both through Federal action and by encouraging the establishment of State programs. The Act authorizes the determination and listing of species as endangered and threatened; prohibits unauthorized taking, possession, sale, and transport of endangered species; provides authority to acquire land for the conservation of listed species, using land and water conservation funds; authorizes establishment of cooperative agreements and grants-in-aid to States that establish and maintain active and adequate programs for endangered and threatened wildlife and plants; and authorizes the assessment of civil and criminal penalties for violating the Act or regulations. Section 7 of the Endangered Species Act requires Federal agencies to ensure that any action authorized, funded or carried out by them is not likely to jeopardize the continued existence of listed species or modify their critical habitat.

Executive Order 12962 – Recreational Fisheries signed on June 7, 1995, mandates that Federal agencies improve the quantity, function, sustainable productivity, and distribution of US aquatic resources for increased recreational fishing opportunities by such activities as: developing and encouraging partnerships between governments and the private sector to advance aquatic resource conservation and enhance recreational fishing opportunities; identifying recreational fishing opportunities that are limited by water quality and habitat degradation and promoting restoration to support viable, healthy, and, where feasible, self-sustaining recreational fisheries; fostering sound aquatic conservation and restoration endeavors to benefit recreational fisheries; supporting outreach programs designed to stimulate angler participation in the conservation and restoration of aquatic systems; and implementing laws under their purview in a manner that will conserve, restore, and enhance aquatic systems that support recreational fisheries. In addition, this order establishes a National Recreational Fisheries Coordination Council which will oversee the various Federal agencies' actions and programs to ensure that they accomplish the goals set forth in this order. Concerning the potential overlap of this order and the Endangered Species Act of 1973 (ESA), all Federal agencies are instructed to aggressively work to identify and minimize conflicts between recreational fisheries and their respective responsibilities under the ESA.

Executive Order 13112 – Invasive Species signed on February 3, 1999, requires Federal agencies, to the extent permitted by law, to prevent the introduction of invasive species and provide for their control, as well as to minimize the economic, ecological, and human health impacts that invasive species cause.

Executive Order 11987 – Exotic Organisms signed on May 24, 1977, requires Federal agencies, to the extent permitted by law, to: restrict the introduction of exotic species into the natural ecosystems on lands and waters owned or leased by the United States; encourage States, local governments, and private citizens to prevent the introduction of exotic species into natural ecosystems of the US; restrict the importation and introduction of exotic species into any natural US ecosystems as a result of activities they undertake, fund, or authorize; and restrict the use of Federal funds, programs, or authorities to export native species for introduction into ecosystems outside the US where they do not occur naturally.

50 CFR 17 – Endangered and Threatened Wildlife and Plants
50 CFR 81 – Conservation of Endangered and Threatened Species of Fish, Wildlife, and Plants (Cooperation with the states)
50 CFR 40 – Endangered Species Act of 1973, as amended (Interagency Cooperation)

Texas Parks and Wildlife

Wildlife Conservation Act (1983) – Texas Legislature placed authority for managing fish and wildlife resources in all Texas counties with the Texas Parks and Wildlife Department when it passed the Wildlife Conservation Act in 1983.

The Texas Parks and Wildlife Code was enacted by §1 of Acts 1975, 64th leg., p. 1405, ch. 545, effective September 1, 1975. Section 2 thereof repealed enumerated articles of the Texas Civil Statutes and Penal Code of 1925 as well as local and special game and fish laws.

The Texas Parks and Wildlife Code provides authority to the Texas Parks and Wildlife Department to conduct scientific surveys of fish and game populations and regulate harvest seasons, bag limits, and means and methods of taking fish and game species. Amended by Acts 1997, 75th Leg, ch. 1256, §1, eff. Sept. 1, 1997.

International Boundary and Water Commission (IBWC)

IBWC responsibilities and obligations include dam operation and management, gauging stations, water quality, hydrologic resources, boundary obstructions, and the power plant. Laws and agreements directing the IBWC's management include the 1944 Water Treaty, 1970 Water Treaty, NEPA (PL 91-190, 40 CFR 1500), TCEQ (337.201, 337.212), Flood Plain Management (E.O. 11988), and the Clean Water Act (PL 92-500, 33 USC 1251-1387).

Mexico

Secretaria de Agricultura, Ganaderia, Desarrollo Rural y Pesca (SAGARPA)
[See Appendix III for organizational structure]

Fishing has been present in Mexico before the conquest, in colonial times, during independence and during the times of the reform (1860s). During the times of the *"Porfiriato"* (1876-1910), the Department of Development, *Secretaria de Fomento*, regulated this activity. In post-revolutionary Mexico (1930-present), the regulation of this activity corresponded first to the Department of Economics, *Secretaría de Economía*, then to the Fishing Undersecretary, *Subsecretaría de Pesca*, of the Department of Commerce, *Secretaria de Comercio*, with the Departments of the Navy and Water resources, *Secretarias de Marina y de Recursos Hicráulicos*, also intervening in the regulation of this activity. In 1976, during the Lopez Portillo administration, all the fishing regulatory functions were placed under the Fishing Division, *Departmento de Pesca*. In 1982 the Fishing Department, *Secretaría de Pesca*, was established and then in 1994, it became part of the Department of the Environment, *Secretaria del Medio Ambiente*. Recently, in December of 2000, the Organic Law of Public Administration mandated that, starting in August 2001, fishing be managed through the National Fishing Commission, *Comisión Nacional de Pesca*.

During the different times that the government has regulated and promoted fishing, several laws and regulations have been passed. Some articles have also been derogated to make fishing more suitable to the prevailing circumstances. The current fishing law, *Ley de Pesca*, was drawn up in June 9, 1992; its by-laws and amendments were published in the daily register, *Diario Oficial*, on September 9, 1999.

The legal framework that regulates fishing activities is formed by laws, by-laws, accords, memorandums, official norms and agreements. However, the Fishing Law, *Ley de Pesca*, is what directly rules this activity.

- The fishing law contains:
  Chapter I – General dispositions.
  Chapter II – Concessions, permits and authorizations.
  Chapter III – Research and training.
  Chapter IV – Inspections, violations and sanctions.

Chapter V – Administration.

- The fishing by-law contains:
  First title – Federal dispositions.
  Second title – General fishing regulations.
  Third title – Aquaculture.
  Fourth title – Termination of permits, concessions and authorizations.
  Fifth title – Inspections, violations and sanctions.
  Sixth title – Impugnation means.

NOM-017-94 regulates sport fishing.
[See this appendix for outline of the Regulatory Process]

NOM-010-PESC-1993 establishes the requirements for the importation of live aquatic animals within national territory. (DOF. 16-VIII-1993). It considers:

- Species of commercial and recreational use.
- Minimum catch sizes
- Quantity and characteristics of the catches.
- Restricted areas to fishing

The National Institute of Fishing, *Instituto Nacional de la Pesca*, is an administrative organization, not under direct control of SAGARPA, whose task is to conduct research to provide the scientific and technical knowledge needed for the proper management and conservation of fishing and aquatic resources and the environment. The *Instituto Nacional de la Pesca* conducts research and oversees the fishery harvest at Amistad.

Mexican Fisheries Regulation Process

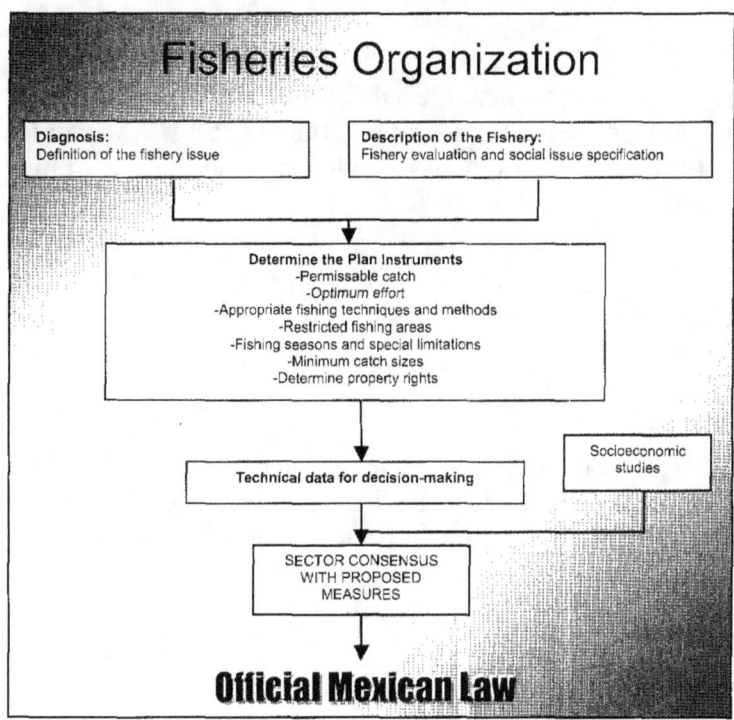

The National Water Law, published in 1992, has for a mission: to regulate the exploitation, the use and benefits, and the distribution and control of the national waters, such as the preservation of quantity and quality. In coordination with SAGARPA, promote the development of aquaculture.

Appendix V. Texas Parks and Wildlife Department's fish stocking criteria

Blue catfish:
1) New or renovated reservoirs where the sale of blue catfish is not legal.
2) Reservoirs with an identified need for an additional sport fish where no blue catfish are present or blue catfish recruitment is inadequate and the sale of blue catfish is not legal.

Bluegill:
1) New or renovated reservoirs.

Channel catfish:
1) New or renovated reservoirs.
2) Urban, community, state park, Wildlife Management Areas, and other TPWD waters ≤75 acres (30 hectares) with insufficient channel catfish recruitment.
3) Waters >75 acres (30 hectares) with insufficient channel catfish recruitment.

Largemouth bass:
1) New or renovated reservoirs.
2) Reservoirs with a significant increase in habitat resulting from increased water level or artificially induced vegetation.
3) Community Fishing Lakes may only be stocked with native largemouth bass.
4) Reservoirs with a history of producing trophy bass, but lacking sufficient numbers of pure FLMB (*Micropterus salmoides floridaus*) (<20% FLMB genotype in electrophoresis samples from age 0 or age 1).
5) Reservoirs which do not have FLMB established (<20% FLMB alleles in electrophoresis samples from age 0 or age 1 fish).

Striped bass:
1) Large mainstream reservoirs.
2) Reservoirs with abundant shad and an existing striped bass fishery.

Palmetto bass (striped bass X white bass):
1) Reservoirs having abundant shad and an existing hybrid striped bass fishery.

Appendix VI. Protocols for implementing new management recommendations

The following are individual agency protocols for implementing new management regulations. These protocols would be applicable to the establishment of any new or changed regulations on Amistad Reservoir under that agency's authorities.

Texas Parks and Wildlife Department regulation process:
- Regulation proposal is submitted by TPWD Fisheries Biologist (or other branch). Proposal is peer reviewed by entire TPWD fisheries staff.
- Regulation proposals are presented at scoping meetings (Regulatory Hearings) held at selected sites statewide, to members of the Texas Freshwater Advisory Board, and to Game Wardens during game warden/biologist meetings. Public input is received, recorded and submitted to TPWD Commissioners.
- Proposals are presented to TPWD Commissioners.
- Special Commissioner's meeting is held where public input is again received. After review, proposals are voted on by Commissioners.
- If approved, regulations become effective following September 1st.

National Park Service regulation process:
Rules applicable to individual units in the National Park Service are found in Title 36, Code of Federal Regulations (CFR), Chapter I. A rule (also called a regulation or rulemaking) is a document to implement or interpret law or policy.

Parks can make new regulations applicable to their areas through the federal regulatory system:
1. A notice of proposed rulemaking must be published in the Federal Register. The proposed rule must set forth the plan/intention for the rule and solicit public comment.
2. The park evaluates the public's comments and, if necessary, modifies the proposal and publishes the final rule in the Federal Register.
3. Once a rule is published in final, it is codified in the Code of Federal Regulations and remains in effect until it is modified by publication of another rule.

The CFR also requires the superintendent to compile in writing all local designations, closures, permit requirements and other restrictions imposed under their discretionary authority, as provided in individual CFR sections.

Mexico regulation process:
The Federal Government of Mexico, in conjunction with the states of Mexico, is in the process of developing regulation implementation protocols and will provide those to the plan in the future along with the Amistad Reservoir Official Mexican Fishing Law (fishing regulations are included on pages 10, 20 and 21).

Appendix VII. Descriptions of future projects/studies at Amistad Reservoir

Project Title: Determine the total economic value of fishery resources of Amistad Reservoir.

Abstract

Amistad Reservoir is one of the largest and most popular bass fishing resources in the state of Texas. The Binational Fisheries Management Plan for Amistad Reservoir has identified that information concerning the economic impact that fishing has on Mexico and Texas is crucial to the proper management and protection of the fisheries resource. An angler survey including an economic analysis has never been conducted at Amistad Reservoir. Conducting this type survey would also provide an opportunity to collect information needed to better understand angler socio-demographic characteristics, attitudes, opinions, and preferences.

Background

Fishing is one of the largest recreational uses of Amistad Reservoir. The trophy bass fishery at Amistad attracts around 150 organized bass tournaments to the reservoir annually. Most tournaments occur on the United States side, but approximately 10 occur on the Mexico side, most involving fishing clubs from Saltillo, the capital of the state of Coahuila, Mexico. The number of fishing tournaments documented on the US side from 2002 to 2006 included the following: 2002= 155, 2003= 156, 2004= 138, 2005= 146, and 2006= 148. At times, when 2 or 3 tournaments occur on the same weekend, there may be as many as 500 tournament boats on the water. The Texas Parks and Wildlife Department considers Amistad Reservoir to be one of the top trophy bass reservoirs in the state of Texas.

One of the highest priorities for the Binational Fisheries Management Plan is to complete an economic analysis of fisheries resources. Many unknowns exist in respect to the financial benefits fishing at Amistad provides to the state of Texas and the state of Coahuila in Mexico. The reservoir was impounded to increase water supply for agriculture, industry, and domestic use; to regulate stream flow and flood control; and to provide for water-based outdoor recreation. Since impoundment, the economic importance of fishing activities to the local area, Mexico, and Texas have increased, but agricultural and municipal uses remain the highest priorities for water resource allocation. In the future, increased demand for water has the potential to reduce water levels, which could negatively affect fish populations, decrease visitation, and reduce the economic impacts that the fisheries resource provides. In order for decision makers to give appropriate consideration to the importance of the fishery resources and water-based recreational activities, an economic analysis is needed to establish the total value of the fishery at Amistad Reservoir. A similar study in Texas showed that Toledo Bend Reservoir had a one-year recreational value of $38 million (Thailing and Ditton 2001).

Need

An economic analysis of fishing activities at Amistad is needed to provide information to local city management, the public and responsible agencies on the importance of

---

maintaining and improving fisheries resources. It was identified as the top priority for the working team involved in developing the Amistad Binational Fisheries Management Plan.

Benefits

The following information will be obtained from an economic analysis of recreational tournament anglers, recreational non-tournament anglers, and commercial anglers on Mexico and United States waters.

- Total direct angler expenditures.
- Total economic impact on the local and state economies of Mexico and the United States.
- Total angler consumer surplus (willingness to pay).
- Total recreational and commercial value of fisheries resources.
- Angler social and demographic characteristics.
- Angler attitudes, opinions, and management preferences.
- Determination of angler feedback on a variety of management scenarios to better meet angler wants and needs and to enhance overall satisfaction.

Description of recommended project

Methods

Conduct an economic analysis of recreational tournament anglers and recreational non-tournament anglers. Request for funding will be sent through SEPAS Natural Resources Program NRPP USGS RESEARCH funding source. Dr. Harold Schramm, Jr., Mississippi Cooperative Fish and Wildlife Research Unit, Mississippi State University and Dr. Robert Ditton, Human Dimensions Research Laboratory, Texas A&M University, Dept. of Wildlife and Fisheries Sciences, are two of the qualified researchers who have been consulted concerning the proposed economic analysis. 0

Budget: See project number two for budget reference.

References

Thailing, Carole and R. Ditton. 2001. Characteristics, participation patterns, attitudes, management preferences, expenditures, and economic impacts of Toledo Bend Reservoir anglers: Texas and Louisiana. Department of Wildlife and Fisheries Sciences, Texas A&M University. College Station, Texas. 174 pages.

Project Title: Creel census of anglers at Amistad Reservoir.

Abstract

Amistad International Reservoir is a multi-purpose reservoir that impounds the Rio Grande and Devils River. The reservoir was completed in 1968 and contains over 800 miles of shoreline and 65,000 shared acres (26,300 hectares) of surface waters between Mexico and the United States. Amistad Reservoir is one of the largest and most popular bass fishing resources in the state of Texas. Agencies involved in the management of fisheries resources for this reservoir include the National Park Service, Texas Parks and Wildlife Department, the United States Fish and Wildlife Service, and the Secretary of Agriculture, Livestock, Rural Development, Fisheries and Nutrition (SAGARPA, Mexico). A one-year international creel census of anglers is needed to estimate the current fishing pressure at Amistad Reservoir and will be used to effectively design an economic analysis to better understand angler socio-demographic characteristics, attitudes, opinions, and preferences.

Statement

The creel census is the first step in a two-year project. The creel census will provide the following information for conducting an economic analysis during the second year of work. During each creel intercept of fishing parties at the lake, a randomly selected angler in each fishing party will be informed of the future study, provided with an information sheet about the project, and asked to cooperate. The objective is to determine an adequate sample size needed for representing local Texas anglers, local Mexican anglers, non-local Texas anglers, non-local Mexican anglers, out-of-state US anglers, and out-of-state Mexican anglers to detect differences in angler expenditures, socio-demographic characteristics, attitudes, opinions, and preferences between these groups.

A creel census will obtain the necessary information for conducting an economic analysis of anglers and tournaments. The following information will be obtained from a creel census.

- Determination of catch and harvest rates and species size distribution.
- Collection of names and addresses of anglers intercepted during census on Mexico and United States waters.
- Determination of sample size to achieve a 95% confidence interval for angler groups.
- Create survey estimates that are representative of the total reservoir boat angler population with a +/- 5% margin of error.

Objectives

- Provide an estimate of fishing effort and the proportion of the effort contributed by local Texas, local Mexican, non-local Texas, non-local Mexican, out-of-state United States, and out-of state Mexican anglers.
- Provide estimates of catch and harvest rates and species size distribution.

Methods

A random access point creel will be conducted across 4 quarters (Spring - March 1 through May, Summer - June 1 through August, Fall - September 1 through November, and Winter - December 1 through February) at Amistad Reservoir on the US and Mexican side. An access point creel design is preferred over a roving creel because of 1) the large size of the reservoir compared to limited number of access points (5), and 2) an access point creel would provide observations of completed versus partial fishing trips.

Creels will be divided into 3-hour morning, 3-hour mid-day, and 3-hour evening creels as well as weekday and weekend creels. A creel schedule generator program will be used to randomly select a minimum of 48 creel days (12 creel days for each quarter). Ramp access site selection, weekend to weekday ratio and seasonal effects will be adjusted based on the proportions estimated by the pre-creel trailer counts. Creel clerks will count all anglers that exit the access points, including those not interviewed. Creel clerks will obtain angler names, addresses, and phone numbers and record fish species, length, weight, catch and harvest information from as many anglers as possible.

Four surveys will be administered. In Texas, the creel clerks will record names, addresses and phone numbers of anglers contacted during creel activities for one year starting in March, 2001. These anglers will receive a survey by mail no more than three months after contact with creel clerks. Also in Texas, tournament rosters of participants in bass tournaments including names, addresses and phone numbers will be obtained from tournament organizers, and these anglers will receive surveys by mail no later than three months following the tournament activity. In Mexico, recreational anglers will be administered an onsite survey during creel activities. A separate survey will be designed and administered to commercial anglers in Mexico. US and Mexican, non-tournament recreational anglers will be checked for duplication of effort.

Budget

Budget Category	Amount (dollars)
In-kind services	
TPWD personnel (creel census)(10 days, @ S25/hour)	$2,000
TPWD (vehicle expenses, creel census)	
(3,000 miles @ .28/mile)	$840
NPS personnel (creel census)	
(1 GS-11, 10 days, @ $25/hour)	$2,000
SAGARPA personnel (creel census)	
(1 staff employee, 10 days, @ $200 a week)	$400
FY-2002 Total Creel In-kind Services	S5,420
Project expenses	
2 clerks @ $9.00/hour for 600 hours	$10,800
Equipment and Supplies	$300
Vehicles 5600 miles @ .28/mile	S1,568
Travel (lodging and per diem)	$2,000
(lodging costs include clerk housing, incidental lodging for TPWD techs.)	
Printing	$500
Communication and postage	$600

Project Title: Conduct cooperative monitoring (studies) of commercial and sport fish populations (TPWD, INP, SAGARPA, NPS).

Abstract

Two types of fisheries currently exist on Amistad Reservoir. A commercial fishery, which consists of harvest by gill nets and trap (hoop) nets, is in place on the Mexico side. A sports fishery, which consists of harvest by rod and reel, jug lines and trotlines, exists on the United States side of the reservoir. Sports fishery on the Mexico side is limited to rod and reel fishing. Commercial fishermen in Mexico target rough fish for part of their catch (carp, gar, freshwater drum and buffalo). Texas Parks and Wildlife Department (TPWD) monitors the relative abundance of rough fish during routine sampling (gill net) on the United States portion of the reservoir. These species are not directly targeted for collection by TPWD.

To determine the relative health of the fisheries found in Amistad Reservoir, various survey techniques need to be implemented. TPWD currently has standardized survey methods designed to sample a particular portion (target species) of the fisheries population. Surveys have been conducted on Amistad by TPWD since it was impounded. Standardized sampling will be continued in order to determine current status of fisheries and develop trend data over time.

Statement

Historically, TPWD has conducted surveys every 3-4 years on Amistad Reservoir. These surveys were conducted only on the United States portion of the reservoir. Under a new agreement with Mexico agencies, sampling will be conducted on the United States and Mexico portions of the reservoir. Sampling sites will be computer-generated random sites. Data will be recorded separately by site to maintain site integrity. Catch per unit of effort by sampling gear and length frequency data will be compared between U.S. sites (where commercial harvest is not permitted) and Mexico sites (where commercial harvest is permitted). To the degree possible, habitat will also be evaluated to determine what affects it may have had on relative species abundance. Other factors that will be considered include species composition, frequency of netting activities per site, type of netting gear utilized per site and possibly total netting pressure for a given area of the reservoir.

Various survey techniques will be implemented to collect data on the overall fisheries population found in Amistad Reservoir. Standardized survey methods currently employed by TPWD include gill net collections, electro-fishing collections, creel surveys, habitat and structure evaluation and basic water sampling.

Gill net surveys will be utilized to evaluate open water species (target species) which include channel catfish, blue catfish, flathead catfish, white bass and striped bass. Gill net data is also used to determine relative abundance of carp, buffalo, freshwater drum and gar.

Electro fishing surveys will be conducted to evaluate shoreline species (target species) which include largemouth bass, sunfish, threadfin shad and gizzard shad. Trap (frame) nets will also be used to target sunfish species and crappie species.

Creel surveys (discussed under Project No. 2)

Water sampling will be conducted to determine temperature, pH, conductivity and dissolved oxygen levels.

Observations will be made to document major changes in habitat structure and abundance.

The monitoring of rough fish and their relative abundance will be continued by TPWD biologists during routine sampling. Trend data will be shared with Mexico biologists to assist them with monitoring the population trends. Trend data will be determined from Catch Per Unit of Effort (CPUE) by gill net sampling in the years Amistad is surveyed by TPWD. TPWD data will be provided to Mexico counterparts.

Methods

Gill nets will be set at 15 randomly selected sites on the United States side of the reservoir. Gill nets will also be set at 5 randomly selected sites on the Mexico side in an area subjected to commercial harvest. Collections will be made in January 2002.

Electro-fishing data will be collected at 24 randomly selected sites on the United States side of the reservoir. Collections will be made in November 2001.

Creel surveys will be conducted from March 2002 through February 2003.

Water sampling and habitat evaluation will be conducted in conjunction with gill net and electro-fishing surveys.

Data on rough fish will be collected by TPWD biologists during scheduled gill net collections. Catch per Unit of Effort (CPUE) recorded as number of fish collected per net-night (one net set overnight) will be calculated for rough fish species.

Budget

In-Kind Services, TPWD Personnel	
Gill Net Collections (12 man days)	$1200
Electro-fishing (20 man days)	$2000
Creel Survey	(Project 2)
Habitat evaluation (6 man days)	$ 600
Per diem	$1500
Vehicles (1500 miles @ .28/mile)	$ 420

Project Title: Develop sport fishing tournament weigh-in facilities.

Abstract

Sport fishing tournaments are an extremely popular recreational activity at Lake Amistad and are vital to the local economy. Some of the larger U.S tournaments will contain as many as 250 boats. Neither the United States nor Mexico side of the reservoir currently have adequate facilities to accommodate these large tournaments. Tournaments usually require participants to hold their fish in live wells and release their catch after a formal weigh-in. The development of better fish weigh-in facilities is needed to reduce fish mortality. This project will result in the development of design and construction specifications for a highly functional tournament landing facility and associated on-site improvements for accommodating parking. One or more tournament landing facilities will then be constructed utilizing lake access/tournament permit fees.

Statement

The number of recreational fishing tournament events at Lake Amistad has increased annually since the mid 1980's and now includes around 150 tournaments per year on the US side of the reservoir alone. Often there are multiple tournaments occurring at the same time. Some of the larger U.S tournaments will contain as many as 250 boats. In

---

the state of Coahuila, Mexico, there are close to 20 hunting, shooting and fishing clubs. Additionally, there are social organizations like the Lions and the Rotary clubs, all of which organize fishing tournaments. It is the right of the sub-delegation of fishing, *Subdelegación de Pesca*, to regulate and control fishing tournaments, in order to contribute to the entertainment and leisure of the population within the state. Approximately 10 tournaments per year currently take place on Mexico's side of the reservoir. There are approximately 70 participants per tournament.

Neither the United States nor Mexico side of the reservoir currently have adequate facilities to accommodate large tournaments. Existing parking areas and boat launch ramps overfill during large tournaments, resulting in negative impacts to the participants and other recreational visitors.

Most of the fishing tournaments conducted on the reservoir involve boats with live-wells and result in the fishermen releasing their catch after a formal "weigh-in" procedure. Development of better facilities for fishermen to weigh-in their fish is needed to reduce fish mortality during these tournaments. Tournament organizers using the Diablo East boat ramp on the United States side currently provide temporary weigh-in facilities in a parking lot, requiring contestants to bring their boats out of the water, transfer their fish to plastic bags, then release the fish down a 200 ft. tube (70 meters) back to the water. Similar approaches to holding a tournament are required in Mexico where adequate weigh-in facilitites are also lacking. A mortality study conducted during a 1998 tournament estimated that 65% of the 2400 fish caught during the tournament died after being released. Many bass tournament organizers, and local, State, Federal and Mexican officials, are interested in reducing fish mortality during these tournaments.

Objectives
- Reduce fish mortality resulting from sport fishing tournaments.
- Improve managing agencies' capability to provide for quality fishing tournaments.

Methods
Advice and collaboration will be sought from the tournament organizers to develop design and construction specifications for a highly functional tournament landing facility and associated on-site improvements for accommodating parking. One or more tournament landing facilities will then be constructed utilizing lake access/tournament permit fees.

Budget

Budget Category	Amount (dollars)
Project Design	$10,000
Facility Construction	$100,000

Project Title: Improve reservoir access (roads and boat ramps) on both sides of the reservoir.

Abstract
The Amistad Reservoir has been in a drought situation since 1993. Development around the reservoir for visitor access has historically been based on high water level access. On August 5, 1998, the reservoir was more than 58 vertical feet (17.7 meters) below conservation pool level. Drought conditions have reduced access on both the United States and Mexico sides. The main boat ramp at Playa Tlaloc is not functional at lower water levels, and most anglers on the Mexico side use non-permanent low water ramps as the alternative. A permanent all water level ramp needs to be developed on the Mexico side of the reservoir. Additional analysis of boat ramp options need to be looked at for the United States side.

Objectives
- Improve low water visitor access for the Amistad Reservoir.
- Develop an all water level boat ramp facility for the Mexico side of the reservoir.
- Improve low water boat ramps on the United States side of the reservoir.

Methods
The low water fishing access on the United States side of the reservoir is considered very good for the lower end of the reservoir; however, the access on the Mexico side of the reservoir is limited to one high-water ramp. The State of Coahuila has considered building an additional ramp. The northwest section of the reservoir on the Mexico side is almost entirely surrounded by private property, and this greatly limits the future potential access of the public. The only general public access area is Playa Tlaloc.

In Mexico, the Secretaria de Comunicaciones y Transporte and the Instituto Estatal de Turismo will evaluated options for developing an all water level ramp. Funding sources will be identified and agency coordination will continue.

The National Park Service will be looking at access on the Pecos River and improving low water access sites used around the park.

Project Title: Develop a common informational fact sheet on boat access, fishing, fees, facilities available, basic regulations, etc.

Abstract
A common informational fact sheet will be developed by SAGARPA, TPWD, and the NPS to assist in angler knowledge of reservoir boat access, fees, facilities available, and basic regulations. The fact sheet will be a one page document with information on US waters on one side and information on Mexico waters on the other side. The fact sheet will also contain information on locations for acquiring fishing licenses and legal length requirements for sport fish. The fact sheet will be updated annually.

Objective
- Develop a common informational fact sheet on boat access, fees, facilities, and basic fishing regulations to educate anglers on legal requirements when fishing Amistad Reservoir.

Methods
The State of Coahuila (Department of Tourism), SAGARPA, TPWD, and the NPS will work cooperatively to develop the one page informational fact sheet. One of the highest priorities will be to provide information on where anglers can acquire Mexico fishing licenses.

Project Title: Establish a common form for recording fishing tournament catches.

Abstract
Amistad Reservoir hosts around 150 bass tournaments a year. Angler catch rates, size of fish, and weight of fish are obtained during tournament activities. It is very important that this information is sent to TPWD, SAGARPA, and the NPS for analysis. Most angler catch information from tournaments is recorded on bass club forms that don't provide consistent data. An official standardized data form for bass tournaments will improve the monitoring of sport fish harvest at Amistad Reservoir.

Objectives
- Maintain and enhance catch rates and quality of recreational sport fishing.
- Monitor harvest by sports anglers.

Methods
SAGARPA, TPWD, and the NPS will establish a one page common form for recording fishing tournament catches on Amistad Reservoir. All cooperating agencies will take necessary procedures to receive approval for the use of the form in the public sector.

Project Title: Develop a common web page and links for public information about the reservoir and its recreational opportunities.

Abstract
SAGARPA, TPWD, NPS and the State of Coahuila all have web pages. There is a need to link all these pages to provide the public with an easy way to access all information available on the reservoir and its recreational opportunities. Developing a common web-page that describes information on boat access, fishing, fees, facilities available, license procedures and locations for purchasing licenses, and basic regulations will further assist in educating anglers at Amistad Reservoir.

Objective
- Improve angler knowledge and ease of access to information on fishing requirements at Amistad Reservoir through a web-based system.

Methods
SAGARPA, TPWD, NPS, and the State of Coahuila will develop links between all current web pages. All web pages will contain a location for information on the Binational Fisheries Management Program. The common informational fact sheet, to be developed in project six, will be placed on all cooperating agencies web pages.

Project Title: Improve the coordination and data sharing of water quality monitoring activities on Amistad Reservoir.

Abstract
Amistad Reservoir is one of the largest and most popular bass fishing resources in the state of Texas. The Binational Fisheries Management Plan for Amistad Reservoir has identified that information concerning water quality is crucial to the proper management and protection of the fisheries resource. Coordination of water quality monitoring between Mexico and the US is needed. Current water quality monitoring programs conducted by CILA, CNA, TCEQ, IBWC, NPS, and USGS needs to be identified. Data available from current water quality monitoring programs needs to be identified and shared amongst cooperating agencies.

Statement
Both the Texas Commission on Environmental Quality (TCEQ) and the US Geological Survey (USGS) have active water quality monitoring programs in and around Amistad Reservoir. Both agencies have conducted sampling in the major tributaries to the reservoir (the Rio Grande, and Pecos and Devils rivers), as well as the Rio Grande below the dam. TCEQ also samples the reservoir at three locations for field parameters, nutrients, chlorophyll and bacteria (Purchase et al, 2001). The USGS sites on the Pecos River and Rio Grande have been part of the Rio Grande NASQAN (National Stream Quality Accounting Network) monitoring program since 1996. These sites are sampled 6 to 8 times a year for a variety of constituents, including nutrients, major ions, water soluble pesticides and trace elements.

Through the Texas Clean Rivers Program (CRP), the IBWC coordinates monitoring activities in the Rio Grande Basin by supporting efforts of monitoring partners including TCEQ, USGS, and the NPS. This program supports special projects, acts as a clearing house for data, provides a point of contact for issues in the Rio Grande Basin and provides annual summary reports (Purchase et al, 2001).

Objectives
- Maintain and enhance quality of recreational sport fishing.
- Maintain a healthy sustainable commercial fishery on the Mexico side of the Amistad Reservoir.

Methods

The cooperating agencies involved directly with the Binational Fisheries Management Plan will begin developing contact information on all water quality monitoring projects being conducted in the watershed of Amistad Reservoir. All information will be referenced and linked to the web page to be developed in Project 8.

Reference

Purchase, C.E., et al., Water Resources Scoping Report. 2001. Technical Report NPS/NRWRD/NRTR-2001/295. Amistad National Recreation Area. National Park Service.

Project Title: Evaluate contamination sources and issues.

Abstract

Cooperating agencies will work together to evaluate contamination sources and issues impacting fishery resources at Amistad Reservoir. Depending on threats, TPWD, NPS, and SAGARPA will work with CILA, CNA, TCEQ, IBWC, and USGS in identifying and resolving possible contamination issues with fishery resources.

Project Statement

Salinity in the Rio Grande above and below Amistad and in the Pecos River has been increasing since at least 1975 (Schertz, 1990). During the growing season, (March 15 to September 15) salinity levels can triple due to irrigation return flows. With increasing salinity in its tributaries, Amistad Reservoir has had rising salinity since 1983 (Miyamoto et al, 1995).

Two studies have looked at trends in metals in sediments. A USGS study analyzed trends using data collected by TCEQ sampling and other assessments between 1970 and 1994 (Lee and Wilson, 1997). This analysis indicates that most trace elements levels appear to be steady, although mercury concentrations are increasing in the Pecos River, the Rio Grande above Amistad, and in Amistad Reservoir. Selenium is also increasing in Amistad Reservoir. The only trace elements with a decreasing trend are copper in Amistad Reservoir and silver in the Pecos River (Lee and Wilson, 1997).

The pollutants DDT, DDE and DDD have been detected at low concentrations in the reservoir, with decreasing levels since the early 1970's, which follows the trend nationwide after the ban on DDT (Lee and Wilson, 1997).

Objectives

- Maintain and enhance quality of recreational sport fishing.
- Maintain a healthy sustainable commercial fishery on the Mexico side of Amistad Reservoir.

Methods
Work with federal and state agencies involved in monitoring water quality and determining contamination threats. Develop list of contamination issues that could potentially impact fishery resources at Amistad Reservoir.

References:
Miyamota, S, L.B. Fenn and D. Swietlik. 1995. Flow, Salts, and Trace Elements in the Rio Grande: A Review, Texas A&M University, Texas Water Resources Institute, TR-169, 30pp.

Lee, R.W. and J.T. Wilson. 1997. Trace Elements and Organic Compounds Associated with Riverbed Sediments in the Rio Grande/Rio Bravo Basin, Mexico and Texas. US Geological Survey Fact Sheet, FS-098-97, 6pp.

Shertz, T.L. 1990. Trends in Water-Quality Data in Texas, US Geological Survey Water Resources Investigations Report 89-4178, 177pp.

Project Title: Determine actual long-term institutional monitoring (INA, TPWD, NPS, SAGARPA).

Project identified for development in 2004-2005.

Project Title: Conduct experimental studies on the effects of commercial nets on sport fishes (INA, SAGARPA).

Project identified for development in 2004-2005.